THE AUSTRALIAN

Women's Weekly
macaroons &biscuits

acp
books

contents

macaroons and biscuits

Biscuits of all types, shapes and sizes are easy to make, providing you follow the recipes carefully. Here are some extra tips to help you bake perfect batches every time.

EQUIPMENT

Bake macaroons, biscuits, cookies, meringues and biscotti on flat oven trays with tiny sides.

• If the sides are over 1cm (½ inch) high, baking and browning of the biscuits will be inadequate and/or uneven. It's better to use the base of an upturned cake pan or baking dish rather than a high-sided tray.

• Some oven trays with non-stick finishes cause biscuits to burn on the bottom, so reduce the oven temperature to stop this from happening. If you have a new tray, do a test run with a few biscuits.

• Rectangular slice (also called slab, bar or lamington) pans vary in size, quality, depth and finishes and can have straight or sloping sides. There's not much difference in their capacities. If the pan is quite full of mixture, the slice will take longer to bake than if the mixture is spread more thinly.

• It's vital to know your oven well; make notes of the baking times and temperatures on the recipes. Most domestic ovens have hot spots, so turn the pans around during baking. Start checking after a third of the baking time has expired, you might have to turn the trays several times to get even baking and browning. If you're using two or three levels of racks, switch the positions of the trays during the baking.

• Other equipment you'll need includes an electric mixer, wooden spoons, plastic or rubber spatulas, a metal spatula, mixing bowls, fine wire racks for cooling, and a sifter.

PREPARING

You should always read every recipe right through before you start to do anything.

• Preparing all the ingredients before you start to mix is best, unless there are cooling or standing times involved, which would give you time to prepare the rest of the recipe.

• Check and adjust shelf positions in the oven before preheating the oven to the correct temperature. If you're unsure about the accuracy of the oven, arrange to have its thermostat checked or, a cheaper option, buy an oven thermometer from a kitchenware shop; leave it in the oven so you can easily check it whenever you like.

• Non-stick pans usually need greasing; mostly a light coating of a cooking-oil spray is enough. If the pan is old or scratched use a heavier coating of spray, or grease with butter. Don't over-grease the trays; excess greasing will attract the heat of the oven and may burn the bottoms of the biscuits and anywhere, such as the corners of the trays, that isn't covered by biscuits.

• Baking paper, also known as parchment paper or baking parchment, can be used instead of greasing, but the paper tends to roll up; a light spray of cooking oil will hold the paper in position. If we suggest using baking paper, then it's for a good reason; often baking paper can be used more than once.

MEASURING

Use the correct measuring spoons and cups for dry ingredients and jugs for liquids.

• Use the blade of a knife or metal spatula to level off dry ingredients in cups and spoons.

• When measuring liquids, check the jug markings carefully as some brands give metric, imperial and cup measures – it's easy to make a mistake by looking at the wrong measurement on the jug.

• Check the ingredient being measured at eye level for accuracy.

• In our recipes we give both cup and weight measurements. If you are using kitchen scales, check them for accuracy using an unopened block of butter.

• Scales are more consistently accurate than cup measures, especially if making a large quantity of biscuits.

The oven temperatures in this book are for conventional ovens; if you have a fan-forced oven decrease the temperature by 10-20 degrees.

MIXING

For the best results, have the ingredients at room temperature, particularly the butter.

• The creaming process means the butter, sugar and egg/s are beaten together using an electric mixer. Most biscuit recipes say 'beat until combined'; don't overbeat the ingredients or the mixture will be too soft and the biscuits will spread too much during baking.

• To start, use low/medium speeds for mixing and don't let the mixture change to a lighter colour. The main exception to this rule is when you're making slices; at times a 'light and fluffy' creamed mixture is needed to achieve a lighter texture.

• Macaroons and meringues are made by beating egg whites until soft peaks form. The beaters and bowl must be very clean (grease-free); the smallest speck of yolk will prevent the whites from beating to a foamy, soft peak. The bowl should be deep so the beaters are at least partly covered by the egg white as they gain volume during beating.

• Place the egg whites in the bowl, turn the mixer to medium speed and beat until the whites become foamy and start to hold their shape. Increase the speed a little and beat until the whites reach the correct stage – usually soft peaks. Beating the egg whites fairly slowly to begin with strengthens them, which gives a better shape.

• Add the sugar, a spoonful at a time, and beat the mixture until all the sugar is dissolved before adding the next batch. Test for sugar grains by feeling a little of the mix between your fingertips.

TESTING

Use the baking times we suggest as a guide only.

• Baking times are affected by many factors, such as the temperature of the room and ingredients, oven temperature, accurate measuring, the mixing of the ingredients, oven rack and tray positions, the material the oven trays and cake pans are made from, and so on.

• To test biscuits and cookies, check them towards the end of the suggested baking time; use the side of your thumb to gently 'push' against the side of one biscuit on the tray, it should feel soft, but if it slides, even slightly, on the tray, the biscuits are done. Remove the biscuits from the oven – cooking biscuits until they're crisp will result in hard dry biscuits – then follow the instructions for cooling.

• Some biscuits are cooled on the trays so they crisp from the heat of the trays, or they could be fragile and need time to settle. More solid biscuits are cooled on wire racks.

• Meringues and macaroons are usually baked slowly; they're done when they feel dry.

• Biscotti are usually baked twice, once in a log shape, which is then cooled and sliced, then returned to the oven to dry out.

• Slices are often cake-like so, if in doubt, use a skewer to test the slice towards the end of the baking time. Some slices are a simple single layer of mixture; don't overbake these as they become dry and hard as they cool. They should feel slightly soft while they're still in the oven; they will firm as they cool. Most slices are cooled in the pan.

STORING

Unfilled biscuits and cookies will keep about a week in an airtight container at room temperature.

• If they soften, which happens in humid or wet weather, they can be re-crisped in the oven. Preheat the oven to 180°C/350°F. Place the biscuits in a single layer on an ungreased oven tray; leave in the oven for about 5 minutes or until they feel dry. Cool on wire racks.

• Filled biscuits soften during storage, but sometimes this makes them better to eat. Most butter, chocolate or cream-based fillings for biscuits need to be stored in an airtight container in the fridge.

• Cream-filled fragile biscuits, such as brandy snaps, meringues and macaroons, should be filled no more than 30 minutes before serving, depending on room temperature.

• Unfilled fragile biscuits, like meringues and macaroons etc, can be stored in an airtight container at room temperature for about a week – providing they are dried out well in the first place.

• Biscotti, once properly dried, will keep for months when stored in an airtight container at a cool room temperature.

• Slices will keep in an airtight container in the fridge or at room temperature, depending on their ingredients, for about a week.

• With the exception of filled fragile biscuits, meringues and macaroons, all biscuits and slices will freeze successfully for at least a month; be sure to pack, layer and handle them gently to avoid any damage.

plain biscuits

chocolate chip cookies

250g (8 ounces) butter, softened
1 teaspoon vanilla extract
¾ cup (165g) caster (superfine) sugar
¾ cup (165g) firmly packed light brown sugar
1 egg
2¼ cups (335g) plain (all-purpose) flour
1 teaspoon bicarbonate of soda (baking soda)
375g (12 ounces) dark chocolate Melts,
  chopped coarsely

1 Preheat oven to 180°C/350°F. Grease oven trays.
2 Beat butter, extract, sugars and egg in small bowl with electric mixer until light and fluffy. Transfer mixture to large bowl; stir in sifted flour and soda, in two batches. Stir in chocolate.
3 Roll tablespoons of mixture into balls; place about 5cm (2 inches) apart on trays. Bake about 15 minutes; cool on trays.
prep + cook time 30 minutes **makes** 36
notes Dark chocolate can be replaced with milk or white chocolate. For choc-nut cookies, replace a third of the chocolate with roasted chopped nuts such as hazelnuts, walnuts, pecans or macadamias. Cookies will keep in an airtight container for up to a week.

mini florentines

¾ cup (120g) sultanas
2 cups (80g) corn flakes
¾ cup (60g) roasted flaked almonds
½ cup (100g) red glacé cherries, quartered
⅔ cup (160ml) sweetened condensed milk
60g (2 ounces) white eating chocolate, melted
60g (2 ounces) dark eating (semi-sweet)
  chocolate, melted

1 Preheat oven to 180°C/350°F. Line oven trays with baking paper.
2 Combine sultanas, corn flakes, nuts, cherries and condensed milk in medium bowl.
3 Drop tablespoons of mixture about 5cm (2 inches) apart on trays. Bake about 5 minutes; cool on trays.
4 Spread the bases of half the florentines with white chocolate; spread remaining florentine bases with dark chocolate. Run fork through chocolate to make waves; stand at room temperature until set.

prep + cook time 25 minutes (+ standing) **makes** 25
note Store florentines in an airtight container in the fridge for up to a week.

anzac biscuits

125g (4 ounces) butter, chopped
2 tablespoons golden syrup or treacle
1 tablespoon water
½ teaspoon bicarbonate of soda (baking soda)
1 cup (220g) firmly packed light brown sugar
½ cup (40g) desiccated coconut
1 cup (90g) rolled oats
1 cup (150g) plain (all-purpose) flour

1 Preheat oven to 160°C/325°F. Line oven trays with baking paper.
2 Stir butter, syrup and the water in large saucepan over low heat until smooth. Remove from heat; stir in soda then remaining ingredients.
3 Roll tablespoons of mixture into balls; place about 5cm (2 inches) apart on trays, flatten slightly. Bake about 20 minutes; cool on trays.
prep + cook time 35 minutes **makes** 25
notes Biscuits should still feel soft when they're cooked; they will firm up as they cool.
Store biscuits in an airtight container for up to a week.

honey jumbles

60g (2 ounces) butter
½ cup (110g) firmly packed dark brown sugar
¾ cup (270g) golden syrup or treacle
1 egg
2½ cups (375g) plain (all-purpose) flour
½ cup (75g) self-raising flour
½ teaspoon bicarbonate of soda (baking soda)
1 teaspoon ground cinnamon
1 teaspoon mixed spice
½ teaspoon ground cloves
2 teaspoons ground ginger
GLACÉ ICING
1 egg white
1½ cups (240g) icing (confectioners') sugar
2 teaspoons plain (all-purpose) flour
1 tablespoon lemon juice, approximately
pink food colouring

1 Preheat oven to 160°C/325°F fan-forced. Grease oven trays.
2 Stir butter, sugar and syrup in medium saucepan, over low heat, until smooth.
3 Transfer mixture to large bowl; cool 10 minutes. Stir in egg then sifted dry ingredients, in two batches. Knead dough on floured surface until dough loses its stickiness, cover; refrigerate 30 minutes.
4 Divide dough into 8 portions. Roll each portion into 2cm (¾ inch) thick sausage; cut each sausage into five 6cm (2¼ inch) lengths. Place about 2.5cm (1 inch) apart on oven trays. Make ends rounded with lightly floured fingers and flatten slightly. Bake jumbles about 15 minutes; cool on trays.
5 Make glacé icing.
6 Spread jumbles with pink and white icing; stand at room temperature until set.
GLACÉ ICING Beat egg white lightly in small bowl; gradually stir in sifted icing sugar and flour, then enough juice to make icing spreadable. Place half the mixture in another small bowl; tint with colouring. Keep icings covered with a damp tea towel while in use so they don't dry out.
prep + cook time 40 minutes
(+ refrigeration and standing) **makes** 40
note Store jumbles in an airtight container for up to a week.

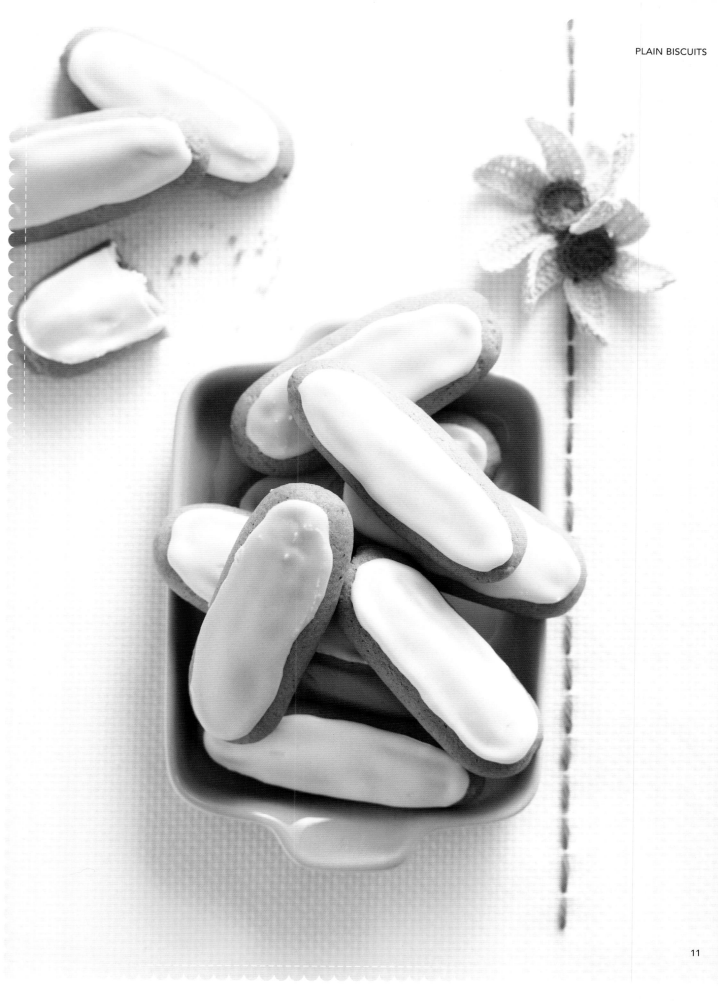

jam drops

125g (4 ounces) butter, softened
½ teaspoon vanilla extract
½ cup (110g) caster (superfine) sugar
1 cup (120g) ground almonds
1 egg
1 cup (150g) plain (all-purpose) flour
1 teaspoon finely grated lemon rind
⅓ cup (110g) raspberry jam (conserve)
2 tablespoons apricot jam (conserve)

1 Preheat oven to 180°C/350°F. Line oven trays with baking paper.
2 Beat butter, extract, sugar and ground almonds in small bowl with electric mixer until light and fluffy. Beat in egg; stir in sifted flour.
3 Divide rind between both jams; mix well.
4 Roll tablespoons of mixture into balls; place about 5cm (2 inches) apart on trays, flatten slightly. Using end of a wooden spoon, press a flower shape, about 1cm (½ inch) deep, into dough; fill each hole with a little jam, using raspberry jam for petals of flowers and apricot jam for centres.
5 Bake drops about 15 minutes. Cool on trays.
prep + cook time 40 minutes **makes** 24
note Jam drops will keep in an airtight container for up to two days.

greek almond crescents

250g (8 ounces) butter, softened
1 teaspoon vanilla extract
1 cup (220g) caster (superfine) sugar
1 egg
¼ cup (60ml) brandy
¾ cup (120g) roasted blanched almonds,
  chopped finely
2½ cups (375g) plain (all-purpose) flour
1½ cups (225g) self-raising flour
½ teaspoon ground nutmeg
¼ cup (60ml) rosewater
½ cup (125ml) water
3 cups (480g) icing (confectioners') sugar

1 Preheat oven to 180°C/350°F. Grease oven trays.
2 Beat butter, extract and caster sugar in small bowl with electric mixer until light and fluffy. Beat in egg and brandy; transfer mixture to large bowl. Stir in nuts and sifted flours and nutmeg, in two batches.
3 Turn dough onto floured surface; knead lightly until smooth. Shape tablespoons of dough into crescent shapes; place about 2.5cm (1 inch) apart on trays. Bake about 15 minutes or until browned lightly.
4 Lift hot crescents onto wire racks; brush with combined rosewater and the water. Coat thickly with sifted icing sugar; cool.
prep + cook time 50 minutes **makes** 50
note Crescents will keep in an airtight container for up to a week.

refrigerator slice & bake cookies

250g (8 ounces) butter, softened
1 cup (160g) icing (confectioners') sugar
2½ cups (375g) plain (all-purpose) flour

1 Beat butter and sifted icing sugar in small bowl with electric mixer until light and fluffy. Transfer to large bowl; stir in sifted flour, in two batches.
2 Knead dough lightly on floured surface until smooth. Divide dough in half; roll each half into a 25cm (10 inch) log. Enclose dough in plastic wrap; refrigerate about 1 hour or until firm.
3 Preheat oven to 180°C/350°F. Grease oven trays.
4 Cut logs into 1cm (½ inch) slices; place 2.5cm (1 inch) apart on trays. Bake about 10 minutes. Cool on trays.

prep + cook time 30 minutes (+ refrigeration)
makes 50
notes These basic cookies can be topped with nuts before baking or, once cooked, iced then dipped into various sprinkles, or simply dusted lightly with sifted icing sugar. If you want to flavour the dough, beat any essence or extract of your choice with the butter and sugar mixture, or beat in a teaspoon or two of the rind of any finely grated citrus fruit. The cookies will keep in an airtight container for at least a week.

chocolate chunk and raspberry cookies

125g (4 ounces) butter, softened
¾ cup (165g) firmly packed light brown sugar
1 egg
1 teaspoon vanilla extract
1 cup (150g) plain (all-purpose) flour
¼ cup (35g) self-raising flour
⅓ cup (35g) cocoa powder
½ teaspoon bicarbonate of soda (baking soda)
90g (3 ounces) dark eating (semi-sweet) chocolate, chopped coarsely
125g (4 ounces) frozen raspberries

1 Preheat oven to 180°C/350°F. Line oven trays with baking paper.
2 Beat butter, sugar, egg and extract in small bowl with electric mixer until combined. Stir in sifted flours, cocoa and soda, in two batches, then stir in chocolate and raspberries.
3 Drop tablespoons of mixture about 5cm (2 inches) apart onto trays; flatten slightly. Bake cookies about 12 minutes. Stand cookies on trays 5 minutes before transferring to a wire rack to cool.
prep + cook time 35 minutes **makes** 24
notes Mix and match different coloured chocolates with different berries if you like. Store cookies in an airtight container in the fridge for up to a week.

malted milk flowers

125g (4 ounces) butter, softened
½ cup (110g) caster (superfine) sugar
1 egg
2 tablespoons golden syrup or treacle
⅓ cup (40g) malted milk powder
2½ cups (375g) plain (all-purpose) flour
½ teaspoon bicarbonate of soda (baking soda)
1½ teaspoons cream of tartar
18 chocolate freckles
18 dark chocolate Melts
MALT ICING
1½ cups (240g) icing (confectioners') sugar
2 tablespoons malted milk powder
2 tablespoons milk, approximately

1 Beat butter, sugar and egg in small bowl with electric mixer until combined, transfer to large bowl; stir in golden syrup and sifted dry ingredients, in two batches. Knead dough lightly on floured surface until smooth. Cover; refrigerate 30 minutes.
2 Preheat oven to 150°C/300°F. Line oven trays with baking paper.
3 Roll dough between sheets of baking paper until 5mm (¼ inch) thick. Cut 7.5cm (3 inch) flowers from dough; place flowers about 2.5cm (1 inch) apart on trays. Bake about 18 minutes. Cool on trays.
4 Meanwhile, make malt icing.
5 Spread biscuits with icing; top half the biscuits with freckles and remaining biscuits with chocolate Melts.
MALT ICING Sift icing sugar and malted milk powder into small heatproof bowl; stir in enough milk to make a thick paste. Stir over small saucepan of simmering water until icing is spreadable.

prep + cook time 50 minutes (+ refrigeration)
makes 36
note Store biscuits in an airtight container for up to a week.

mandarin polenta biscuits

125g (4 ounces) butter, softened
2 teaspoons finely grated mandarin rind
⅔ cup (110g) icing (confectioners') sugar
⅓ cup (55g) polenta
1½ cups (225g) plain (all-purpose) flour
¼ cup (60ml) mandarin juice

1 Preheat oven to 180°C/350°F. Line oven trays with baking paper.
2 Beat butter, rind and sifted icing sugar in small bowl with electric mixer until combined; stir in polenta, sifted flour and juice, in two batches.
3 Shape dough into a 30cm (12 inch) rectangular log. Wrap in plastic; refrigerate 30 minutes.
4 Remove plastic from log; cut log into 1cm (½ inch) slices. Place slices about 2.5cm (1 inch) apart on trays; bake about 15 minutes. Stand biscuits 5 minutes before transferring to wire rack to cool.
prep + cook time 40 minutes (+ refrigeration)
makes 30
notes You will need 2 mandarins for this recipe. Store biscuits in an airtight container for up to a week.

mocha vanilla twists

125g (4 ounces) butter, softened
½ cup (110g) caster (superfine) sugar
1 egg
1 teaspoon vanilla extract
1⅔ cups (250g) plain (all-purpose) flour
2 teaspoons instant coffee granules
2 teaspoons boiling water
2 tablespoons cocoa powder

1 Preheat oven to 180°C/350°F. Line oven trays with baking paper.
2 Beat butter, sugar, egg and extract in small bowl with electric mixer until combined; stir in sifted flour, in two batches.
3 Divide dough in half. Stir combined coffee and the water and sifted cocoa into one portion to make mocha dough.
4 Divide both dough portions into four equal pieces. Roll each portion into a 40cm (16 inch) sausage. Twist one plain sausage and one mocha sausage together; cut into seven 5cm (2 inch) lengths. Repeat with remaining plain and mocha dough.
5 Place twists about 2.5cm (1 inch) apart on trays; bake about 15 minutes. Cool on trays.
prep + cook time 45 minutes **makes** 28
note Store twists in an airtight container for up to a week.

banana, caramel and date cookies

125g (4 ounces) butter, softened
1 cup (220g) firmly packed light brown sugar
1 egg yolk
⅓ cup (100g) mashed banana
2 cups (300g) plain (all-purpose) flour
½ teaspoon bicarbonate of soda (baking soda)
½ cup (75g) finely chopped seeded dried dates
18 chewy toffees, halved

1 Preheat oven to 180°C/350°F. Line oven trays with baking paper.
2 Beat butter, sugar and egg yolk in small bowl with electric mixer until combined, transfer to large bowl; stir in banana, then sifted flour and soda, and dates.
3 Roll tablespoons of mixture into balls; push a piece of toffee into centre of each ball, roll to enclose toffee. Place balls about 5cm (2 inches) apart on trays. Bake about 20 minutes; cool on trays.
prep + cook time 45 minutes **makes** 36
note Store cookies in an airtight container for up to a week.

choc-vanilla noughts & crosses

125g (4 ounces) butter, softened
½ cup (110g) caster (superfine) sugar
1 egg
1 teaspoon vanilla extract
1⅔ cups (250g) plain (all-purpose) flour
2 tablespoons cocoa powder
2 teaspoons milk
⅓ cup (50g) white Choc Bits
⅓ cup (50g) dark Choc Bits

1 Preheat oven to 180°C/350°F. Line oven trays with baking paper.
2 Beat butter, sugar, egg and extract in small bowl with electric mixer until combined; stir in sifted flour, in two batches.

3 Divide dough in half. Stir sifted cocoa and milk into one portion. Cover; refrigerate dough 30 minutes.
4 Roll dough portions, separately, between sheets of baking paper until 5mm (¼ inch) thick. Cut 15 x 6cm (2¼ inch) rounds from each; place about 2.5cm (1 inch) apart on trays.
5 Press white chocolate on chocolate rounds to make crosses; press dark chocolate on vanilla rounds to make noughts. Bake about 15 minutes; cool on trays.
prep + cook time 40 minutes (+ refrigeration)
makes 30
notes You need 96 white and 96 dark Choc Bits to make the noughts and crosses for these biscuits. Store biscuits in an airtight container for up to a week.

coconut sesame crisps

1 teaspoon honey
20g butter
1 egg white
2 tablespoons caster (superfine) sugar
2 tablespoons plain (all-purpose) flour
1 tablespoon desiccated coconut
2 teaspoons sesame seeds

1 Stir honey and butter in small saucepan over low heat until smooth; cool.
2 Preheat oven to 160°C/325°F. Line two oven trays with baking paper; mark four 7.5cm (3 inch) circles on paper on each tray, turn paper over.
3 Beat egg white in small bowl with electric mixer until soft peaks form; gradually add sugar, beating until dissolved. Fold in sifted flour and butter mixture.

4 Spread level teaspoons of mixture to fill centre of each circle on trays; sprinkle with combined coconut and seeds.
5 Bake one tray of crisps at a time for about 5 minutes. Remove crisps from tray immediately using metal spatula; place crisps over rolling pin to cool.
prep + cook time 1 hour **makes** 28
notes You may find it easier to bake just two crisps on a tray at a time. Re-use the baking-paper lining. Store crisps in an airtight container for up to a week.

peanut crunch cookies

¾ cup (110g) self-raising flour
¼ teaspoon bicarbonate of soda (baking soda)
½ teaspoon ground cinnamon
½ cup (45g) rolled oats
⅓ cup (25g) desiccated coconut
1 teaspoon finely grated lemon rind
½ cup (140g) crunchy peanut butter
¾ cup (165g) caster (superfine) sugar
1 tablespoon golden syrup or treacle
2 tablespoons cold water, approximately

1 Process flour, soda, cinnamon, oats, coconut, rind and peanut butter until crumbly; add sugar, golden syrup and enough of the water to make a firm dough. Knead dough lightly on floured surface until smooth; cover, refrigerate 30 minutes.
2 Preheat oven to 180°C/350°F. Grease oven trays.
3 Divide dough in half; roll each half between sheets of baking paper to 5mm (¼ inch) thickness. Cut dough into 6cm (2¼ inch) rounds; place on trays 2.5cm (1 inch) apart. Bake about 10 minutes. Stand biscuits on trays 5 minutes before transferring to a wire rack to cool.
prep + cook time 35 minutes (+ refrigeration)
makes 30
note Store cookies in an airtight container for up to a week.

basic shortbread dough >

Beat 250g (8 ounces) softened butter, ¼ cup caster (superfine) sugar and 1 teaspoon vanilla extract in small bowl with electric mixer until smooth. Transfer to large bowl; stir in 1½ cups sifted plain (all-purpose) flour, in two batches.
prep time 15 minutes **makes** 1 quantity

< choc-mint shortbreads

Finely chop 2 x 35g (1 ounce) Peppermint Crisp bars. Preheat oven to 180°C/350°F. Line oven trays with baking paper. Make 1 quantity basic shortbread dough (see above), replacing caster (superfine) sugar with ¼ cup firmly packed light brown sugar. Stir in 2 tablespoons cocoa powder sifted with a pinch of bicarbonate of soda (baking soda). Roll level tablespoons of mixture into balls. Place balls about 5cm (2 inches) apart onto trays; flatten with the back of a spoon. Bake about 15 minutes; immediately sprinkle hot biscuits with chopped Peppermint Crisp bars. Cool on trays.
prep + cook time 35 minutes **makes** 24

latte shortbread dippers >

Preheat oven to 160°C/325°F. Line oven trays with baking paper. Make 1 quantity basic shortbread dough (see pg 24). Dissolve 4 teaspoons instant coffee granules in 1 teaspoon boiling water; stir coffee mixture into dough. Spoon mixture into piping bag fitted with a 2cm (¾ inch) fluted tube. Pipe 6cm (2¼ inch) lengths about 2.5cm (1 inch) apart onto trays; sprinkle with 1 tablespoon demerara or white (granulated) sugar. Bake about 15 minutes; cool on trays.

prep + cook time 40 minutes **makes** 32

< ginger, lime and cashew shortbreads

Preheat oven to 160°C/325°F. Line oven trays with baking paper. Make 1 quantity basic shortbread dough (see pg 24). Stir in 2 teaspoons finely grated lime rind, 2 tablespoons finely chopped glacé ginger, ¾ cup ground almonds, 2 teaspoons ground ginger and ¼ cup finely chopped roasted unsalted cashews. Shape level tablespoons of mixture into mounds about 2.5cm (1 inch) apart on trays; top each mound with a whole roasted unsalted cashew. Bake about 25 minutes; cool on trays.

prep + cook time 50 minutes **makes** 30

golden oaty carrot cookies

125g (4 ounces) butter, softened
1 cup (220g) firmly packed light brown sugar
1 egg yolk
½ cup (70g) firmly packed coarsely grated carrot
1½ cups (225g) plain (all-purpose) flour
½ teaspoon bicarbonate of soda (baking soda)
1 teaspoon ground cinnamon
1 cup (90g) rolled oats
1 tablespoon milk, approximately

1 Preheat oven to 180°C/350°F. Line oven trays with baking paper.
2 Beat butter, sugar and egg yolk in small bowl with electric mixer until combined. Stir in carrot, then sifted flour, soda and cinnamon. Stir in oats and enough milk to make a firm dough.
3 Roll heaped teaspoons of mixture into balls. Place balls about 5cm (2 inches) apart on trays; flatten slightly. Bake about 15 minutes; cool on trays.
prep + cook time 35 minutes **makes** 44
note Store cookies in an airtight container for up to a week.

gingerbread

125g (4 ounces) unsalted butter, softened
½ cup (110g) firmly packed dark brown sugar
1 egg yolk
2½ cups (375g) plain (all-purpose) flour
1 teaspoon bicarbonate of soda (baking soda)
3 teaspoons ground ginger
½ cup (175g) golden syrup
1 tablespoon pink round sprinkles
ROYAL ICING
1 egg white
1½ cups (240g) pure icing (confectioners') sugar
4 drops lemon juice
yellow and pink food colouring

1 Preheat oven to 180°C/350°F. Line oven trays with baking paper.
2 Beat butter, sugar and egg yolk in small bowl with electric mixer until smooth; transfer to large bowl. Stir in sifted dry ingredients and syrup in two batches.
3 Knead dough gently on floured surface until smooth. Divide dough in half; roll each half between sheets of baking paper to 5mm (¼ inch) thickness. Cut dough into 6 x 12cm (4½ inch) girl shapes, 6 x 12cm (4½ inch) boy shapes and 12 x 6cm (2¼ inch) flower shapes; place on trays 2.5cm (1 inch) apart. Bake about 10 minutes. Cool on trays.

4 Meanwhile, make royal icing.
5 Using picture as a guide, pipe icing onto biscuits using the three different colours; sprinkle centres of flowers with pink sprinkles. Set at room temperature.
ROYAL ICING Beat egg white in small bowl with electric mixer; gradually beat in sifted icing sugar. When mixture reaches piping consistency, beat in juice. Divide icing between three bowls; tint one bowl with yellow colouring and another with pink colouring; leave the remaining bowl plain.
prep + cook time 50 minutes **makes** 24
notes Gingerbread can be stored in an airtight container for at least a week.
You can cut out any shapes you like from the dough. Be careful not to overcook the shapes, they should still feel soft when they're cooked; they become crisp on cooling.

peanut praline cookies

125g (4 ounces) butter, softened
¼ cup (70g) crunchy peanut butter
½ cup (110g) firmly packed light brown sugar
1 egg
1½ cups (225g) plain (all-purpose) flour
½ teaspoon bicarbonate of soda (baking soda)
PEANUT PRALINE
¾ cup (100g) roasted unsalted peanuts
½ cup (110g) caster (superfine) sugar
2 tablespoons water

1 Make peanut praline.
2 Preheat oven to 160°C/325°F. Line oven trays with baking paper.
3 Beat butter, peanut butter, sugar and egg in small bowl with electric mixer until combined. Stir in sifted dry ingredients and half the crushed peanut praline.

4 Roll tablespoons of mixture into balls; place on trays about 5cm (2 inches) apart, flatten slightly. Sprinkle with remaining praline. Bake about 20 minutes. Cool on trays.
PEANUT PRALINE Place peanuts on baking paper-lined oven tray. Combine sugar and the water in small frying pan, stir over heat, without boiling, until sugar is dissolved. Bring to the boil; boil, uncovered, without stirring, until mixture turns a golden brown. Pour mixture over nuts; stand at room temperature until set. Process until coarsely crushed.
prep + cook time 45 minutes (+ standing) **makes** 28
notes Store cookies in an airtight container for up to a week. To save time, use 250g purchased peanut brittle instead of the praline.

amaretti

1 cup (120g) ground almonds
1 cup (220g) caster (superfine) sugar
2 egg whites
¼ teaspoon almond extract
20 blanched almonds (20g)

1 Grease oven trays.
2 Beat ground almonds, sugar, egg whites and extract in small bowl with electric mixer for 3 minutes; stand 5 minutes.
3 Spoon mixture into piping bag fitted with 1cm (½ inch) plain tube. Pipe mixture onto trays in circular motion, from centre out, until about 4cm (1½ inches) in diameter. Top each amaretti with a nut, cover unbaked amaretti loosely with foil; stand at room temperature overnight (see note).
4 Preheat oven to 180°C/350°F.
5 Bake amaretti about 12 minutes. Stand on trays 5 minutes before transferring to a wire rack to cool.

prep + cook time 30 minutes (+ standing) **makes** 20
notes These biscuits are best if the mixture stands overnight: they will work if they're baked straight away, but they're just not quite as good. Amaretti will keep in an airtight container for at least a week.

traditional shortbread

250g (8 ounces) butter, softened
⅓ cup (75g) caster (superfine) sugar
1 tablespoon water
2 cups (300g) plain (all-purpose) flour
½ cup (90g) rice flour
2 tablespoons white (granulated) sugar

1 Preheat oven to 160°C/325°F. Grease oven trays.
2 Beat butter and caster sugar in medium bowl with electric mixer until light and fluffy; stir in the water and sifted flours, in two batches. Knead mixture on floured surface until smooth.
3 Divide mixture in half; shape each half on separate trays into 20cm (8 inch) rounds. Mark each round into 12 wedges; prick with fork. Pinch edges of rounds with fingers; sprinkle shortbread with white sugar.
4 Bake about 40 minutes; stand 5 minutes. Using sharp knife, cut into wedges along marked lines. Cool on trays.
prep + cook time 1 hour **makes** 24
notes Ground white rice can be used instead of rice flour, although it is slightly coarser in texture. Store shortbread in an airtight container for up to a week.

chocolate wheaties

90g (3 ounces) butter, softened
½ cup (110g) firmly packed light brown sugar
1 egg
¼ cup (20g) desiccated coconut
⅓ cup (35g) wheat germ
⅔ cup (100g) wholemeal plain (all-purpose) flour
⅓ cup (50g) white self-raising flour
185g (6 ounces) dark eating (semi-sweet)
  chocolate, melted

1 Beat butter and sugar in small bowl with electric mixer until smooth; add egg, beat until combined. Stir in coconut, wheat germ and sifted flours.
2 Roll dough between sheets of baking paper until 5mm (¼ inch) thick. Place on tray; refrigerate 30 minutes.

3 Preheat oven to 180°C/350°F. Line oven trays with baking paper.
4 Cut 7.5cm (3 inch) rounds from dough; place rounds about 2.5cm (1 inch) apart on trays. Bake about 20 minutes. Cool on trays.
5 Spread bases of wheaties with chocolate; mark with a fork. Stand at room temperature until set.
prep + cook time 50 minutes
(+ refrigeration and standing) **makes** 18
note If the weather is cool, store biscuits in an airtight container at room temperature – refrigerate them if the weather is hot.

golden syrup peanut swirls >

Preheat oven to 180°C/350°F. Line oven trays with baking paper. Make 1 quantity basic shortbread dough (see pg 24) replacing vanilla extract with 1 tablespoon golden syrup or treacle. Stir ¼ cup smooth peanut butter into dough. Spoon mixture into piping bag fitted with a 2cm (¾ inch) fluted tube; pipe 5cm (2 inch) stars about 2.5cm (1 inch) apart onto trays. Bake about 10 minutes; cool on trays.

prep + cook time 30 minutes **makes** 60

< white-choc and cranberry shortbreads

Preheat oven to 180°C/350°F. Line oven trays with baking paper. Make 1 quantity basic shortbread dough (see pg 24). Stir ¼ cup finely chopped dried cranberries and 90g (3 ounces) coarsely grated white eating chocolate into dough. Drop tablespoons of mixture about 5cm (2 inches) apart onto trays. Bake about 15 minutes; cool on trays. Melt 90g (3 ounces) white chocolate Melts; tint pink with food colouring. Drizzle chocolate over biscuits; stand at room temperature until set.

prep + cook time 45 minutes **makes** 26

baklava twists >

Combine ⅔ cup finely chopped roasted unsalted pistachios, 2 tablespoons honey and 3 teaspoons rosewater in small bowl. Preheat oven to 180°C/350°F. Line oven trays with baking paper. Make 1 quantity basic shortbread dough (see pg 24). Stir 2 teaspoons rosewater into dough. Roll rounded teaspoons of mixture into balls; roll balls into 12cm (4½ inch) log. Twist each log into a loop, overlapping one end over the other. Place twists about 2.5cm (1 inch) apart on trays. Top each twist with about ½ teaspoon nut mixture. Bake about 10 minutes; cool on trays.

prep + cook time 45 minutes **makes** 42

filled biscuits

monte carlos

185g (6 ounces) butter, softened
1 teaspoon vanilla extract
½ cup (110g) firmly packed light brown sugar
1 egg
1¼ cups (185g) self-raising flour
¾ cup (110g) plain (all-purpose) flour
½ cup (40g) desiccated coconut
¼ cup (80g) raspberry jam (conserve)
CREAM FILLING
60g (2 ounces) butter
½ teaspoon vanilla extract
¾ cup (120g) icing (confectioners') sugar
2 teaspoons milk

1 Preheat oven to 180°C/350°F. Grease oven trays.
2 Beat butter, extract, sugar and egg in small bowl with electric mixer until smooth. Transfer mixture to large bowl, stir in sifted flours and coconut in two batches. Roll rounded teaspoons of mixture into oval shapes; place about 2.5cm (1 inch) apart on trays. Flatten slightly; rough surface with fork. Bake biscuits about 12 minutes. Cool on wire racks.
3 Make cream filling.
4 Sandwich biscuits with jam and filling.
CREAM FILLING Beat butter, extract and sifted icing sugar in small bowl with electric mixer until light and fluffy; beat in milk.
prep + cook time 1 hour **makes** 25
notes Unfilled biscuits will keep in an airtight container for up to a week. Filled biscuits will keep for a few days in an airtight container in the fridge.

melting moments

250g (8 ounces) butter, softened
1 teaspoon vanilla extract
½ cup (80g) icing (confectioners') sugar
1½ cups (225g) plain (all-purpose) flour
½ cup (75g) cornflour (cornstarch)
BUTTER CREAM
90g (3 ounces) butter
¾ cup (120g) icing (confectioners') sugar
1 teaspoon finely grated lemon rind
1 teaspoon lemon juice

1 Preheat oven to 160°C/325°F. Line oven trays with baking paper.
2 Beat butter, extract and sifted icing sugar in small bowl with electric mixer until light and fluffy. Transfer mixture to large bowl, stir in sifted flours in two batches.

3 With floured hands, roll rounded teaspoons of mixture into balls; place about 2.5cm (1 inch) apart on trays. Flatten slightly with a floured fork.
4 Bake biscuits about 15 minutes. Stand 5 minutes before lifting onto wire racks to cool.
5 Make butter cream.
6 Sandwich biscuits with butter cream. Dust with extra sifted icing sugar before serving, if you like.
BUTTER CREAM Beat butter, sifted icing sugar and rind in small bowl with electric mixer until pale and fluffy; beat in juice.
prep + cook time 40 minutes **makes** 25
notes Unfilled biscuits will keep in an airtight container for up to a week. Filled biscuits will keep for a few days in an airtight container in the fridge.

brandy snaps

90g (3 ounces) butter
½ cup (110g) firmly packed dark brown sugar
⅓ cup (115g) golden syrup or treacle
1 teaspoon ground ginger
⅔ cup (100g) plain (all-purpose) flour
1 teaspoon lemon juice
1¼ cups (300ml) thickened (heavy) cream,
  whipped

1 Preheat oven to 180°C/350°F. Grease oven trays.
2 Stir butter, sugar, syrup and ginger in medium
saucepan, over low heat, until smooth. Remove from
heat; stir in sifted flour and juice.
3 Drop rounded teaspoons of mixture about
5cm (2 inches) apart onto trays. Using a wet, thin
metal spatula, spread mixture into 8cm rounds.

Bake about 8 minutes or until snaps are bubbling
and golden brown.
4 Slide a thin metal spatula under each snap; quickly
shape each one into a cone. Place snaps on wire rack
to cool. Fill with whipped cream just before serving.
prep + cook time 40 minutes **makes** 32
notes Brandy is not an ingredient in brandy snaps
today, but was possibly included many years ago. If
you like, add a little icing sugar and a tablespoon of
brandy to the whipped cream.
Bake the first tray of snaps and while they are cooking
prepare the next tray of snaps; put them into the oven
as you're getting the first batch out. If you handle four
snaps at a time, the process will be easy. Snaps are
best made on the day of serving.

chocolate caramel shortbread cookies

18 round shortbread biscuits (360g) (see notes)
185g (6 ounces) dark eating chocolate,
  chopped coarsely
2 teaspoons vegetable oil
CARAMEL FILLING
½ cup (110g) firmly packed light brown sugar
60g (2 ounces) butter, chopped
2 teaspoons water
1½ tablespoons cornflour (cornstarch)
½ cup (125ml) milk
1 egg yolk
1 teaspoon vanilla extract

1 Make caramel filling.
2 Spread caramel filling over half of the shortbread biscuits; top with remaining biscuits. Cover, refrigerate 1 hour.
3 Melt chocolate in small heatproof bowl over saucepan of simmering water (do not allow water to touch base of bowl). Remove from heat; stir in oil.

4 Dip one side of cookies in melted chocolate. Stand at room temperature until set.
CARAMEL FILLING Combine sugar, butter and the water in small saucepan; stir over heat until sugar is dissolved. Stir in blended cornflour and milk; stir over heat until mixture boils and thickens. Remove from heat; whisk in egg yolk and extract. Carefully cover surface of caramel with plastic wrap, refrigerate 3 hours or overnight.
prep + cook time 25 minutes (+ refrigeration)
makes 9
notes You will need 3 x 120g (4 ounce) packets round shortbread biscuits for this recipe. The biscuits should be 6cm (2¼ inches) in diameter. Store filled and chocolate-dipped cookies in an airtight container in the fridge for up to a week.

lime and ginger kisses

125g (4 ounces) butter, softened
½ cup (110g) firmly packed light brown sugar
1 egg
¼ cup (35g) plain (all-purpose) flour
¼ cup (35g) self-raising flour
¾ cup (110g) cornflour (cornstarch)
2 teaspoons ground ginger
½ teaspoon ground cinnamon
¼ teaspoon ground cloves
LIME BUTTER CREAM
60g (2 ounces) butter, softened
2 teaspoons finely grated lime rind
¾ cup (120g) icing (confectioners') sugar
2 teaspoons milk

1 Preheat oven to 180°C/350°F. Line oven trays with baking paper.
2 Beat butter, sugar and egg in small bowl with electric mixer until smooth. Stir in sifted dry ingredients.
3 Roll heaped teaspoons of mixture into balls; place balls about 5cm (2 inches) apart on trays. Bake about 10 minutes. Loosen biscuits; cool on trays.
4 Make lime butter cream. Sandwich biscuits with butter cream.
LIME BUTTER CREAM Beat butter and rind in small bowl with electric mixer until as white as possible. Beat in sifted icing sugar and milk, in two batches.
prep + cook time 35 minutes (+ cooling) **makes** 18
notes Unfilled biscuits will keep in an airtight container for up to a week. Filled biscuits will keep for a few days in an airtight container in the fridge.

rosewater meringue kisses >

Preheat oven to 120°C/250°F. Grease oven trays; line with baking paper. Beat 2 egg whites, ½ cup caster (superfine) sugar, 1 teaspoon rosewater and few drops pink food colouring in small bowl with electric mixer about 15 minutes or until sugar is dissolved. Spoon mixture into piping bag fitted with 2cm (¾ inch) fluted tube; pipe 4cm (1½ inch) stars onto trays 2cm (¾ inch) apart. Bake about 1 hour. Cool on trays. Meanwhile, bring 2 tablespoons pouring cream to the boil in small saucepan. Remove from heat; add 90g (3 ounces) finely chopped white eating chocolate; stir until smooth. Stir in 2 teaspoons pureed strained raspberries and few drops pink food colouring. Refrigerate 20 minutes or until spreadable. Sandwich meringues with filling.
prep + cook time 1 hour 25 minutes
(+ cooling and refrigeration) **makes** 20

< mocha hazelnut meringues

Preheat oven to 120°C/250°F. Grease oven trays; line with baking paper. Beat 3 egg whites in small bowl with electric mixer until soft peaks form. Gradually add ¾ cup caster (superfine) sugar, beating until dissolved between additions. Dissolve 2 teaspoons instant coffee granules and 2 teaspoons cocoa powder in 2 teaspoons hot water in small heatproof jug; stir in 2 teaspoons hazelnut-flavoured liqueur. Fold coffee mixture into meringue mixture. Spoon meringue into piping bag fitted with 1cm (½ inch) plain tube. Pipe 50 x 1cm (½ inch) shapes onto trays; top each with 1 whole roasted hazelnut. Pipe remaining meringue over hazelnuts to enclose. Bake about 45 minutes. Cool on trays. Dip one side of meringues in 180g (6 ounces) melted dark eating chocolate; stand at room temperature to set.
prep + cook time 1 hour 10 minutes
(+ cooling and standing) **makes** 50

choc-orange meringues >

Preheat oven to 120°C/250°F. Grease oven trays; line with baking paper. Beat 3 egg whites in small bowl with electric mixer until soft peaks form. Gradually add ¾ cup caster (superfine) sugar, beating until dissolved between additions. Fold 1 tablespoon sifted cocoa powder, 2 teaspoons finely grated orange rind and 2 teaspoons orange-flavoured liqueur into meringue mixture. Drop level tablespoons of mixture onto trays 2cm (¾ inch) apart. Bake about 1 hour. Cool on trays. Drizzle meringues with 90g (3 ounces) melted dark eating chocolate; stand at room temperature until set.

prep + cook time 1 hour 25 minutes (+ cooling and standing) **makes** 50

< choc-mint meringues

Preheat oven to 120°C/250°F. Grease oven trays; line with baking paper. Beat 2 egg whites and ½ cup caster (superfine) sugar in small bowl with electric mixer about 15 minutes or until sugar is dissolved; fold in 2 tablespoons sifted cocoa powder. Spoon mixture into piping bag fitted with 2cm (¾ inch) fluted tube; pipe 4cm (1½ inch) stars onto trays 2cm (¾ inch) apart. Bake about 1 hour. Cool on trays. Beat 60g (2 ounces) butter in small bowl with electric mixer, beat in ½ cup sifted icing (confectioners') sugar, 2 teaspoons milk and ½ teaspoon peppermint extract. Sandwich meringues with peppermint filling; dust with extra sifted cocoa powder before serving, if you like.

prep + cook time 1 hour 25 minutes (+ cooling) **makes** 18

spicy fruit mince pillows

90g (3 ounces) butter, softened
⅓ cup (55g) icing (confectioners') sugar
1 egg
1¼ cups (185g) plain (all-purpose) flour
¼ cup (35g) self-raising flour
2 tablespoons milk
2 teaspoons caster (superfine) sugar
SPICY FRUIT FILLING
2⅔ cups (375g) seeded dried dates,
   chopped coarsely
¾ cup (180ml) water
2 teaspoons ground allspice
¼ teaspoon ground cloves
pinch bicarbonate of soda (baking soda)

1 Beat butter and sifted icing sugar in small bowl with electric mixer until smooth. Beat in egg until combined. Stir in sifted flours, in two batches. Cover dough; refrigerate 30 minutes.
2 Meanwhile, make spicy fruit filling.
3 Preheat oven to 180°C/350°F. Line oven trays with baking paper.
4 Roll dough between sheets of baking paper to 30cm x 40cm (12 inch x 16 inch) rectangle; cut into four 7.5cm (3 inch) x 40cm (16 inch) strips. Spoon filling into piping bag fitted with large 1.5cm (¾ inch) plain tube; pipe filling down centre of each strip. Fold edges in until they meet to enclose filling; turn seam-side down onto board. Cut each roll into 10 pillow shapes; place pillows, seam-side down, on trays; brush with milk, sprinkle with caster sugar.
5 Bake pillows about 20 minutes; cool on trays.
SPICY FRUIT FILLING Combine dates and the water in medium saucepan; cook, stirring, about 10 minutes or until thick and smooth. Stir in spices and soda. Cool.
prep + cook time 50 minutes (+ refrigeration)
makes 40
note Pillows will keep in an airtight container at room temperature for up to a week.

caramel peanut hearts

125g (4 ounces) butter, softened
½ cup (110g) caster (superfine) sugar
1 tablespoon golden syrup or treacle
⅓ cup (95g) crunchy peanut butter
1½ cups (225g) plain (all-purpose) flour
⅓ cup (80ml) caramel top 'n' fill
1 tablespoon icing (confectioners') sugar

1 Beat butter, sugar, golden syrup and peanut butter in small bowl with electric mixer until combined. Stir in sifted flour, in two batches. Cover dough; refrigerate 30 minutes.
2 Preheat oven to 180°C/350°F. Line oven trays with baking paper.

3 Roll dough between sheets of baking paper until 5mm (¼ inch) thick; cut 32 x 7.5cm (3 inch) hearts from dough. Place hearts about 2.5cm (1 inch) apart on trays. Cut 2.5cm (1 inch) hearts from centres of 16 large hearts.
4 Bake whole hearts about 10 minutes and remaining hearts about 8 minutes; cool on trays.
5 Spread whole hearts with caramel; top with remaining hearts. Dust hearts with sifted icing sugar.
prep + cook time 1 hour
(+ refrigeration and cooling) **makes** 16
notes Unfilled biscuits will keep in an airtight container for up to a week. Filled biscuits will keep for a few days in an airtight container in the fridge.
Caramel top 'n' fill is a thick caramel, suitable to use in pie fillings, etc. It is available from supermarkets.

choc-cranberry chews

90g (3 ounces) butter, softened
¼ cup (55g) caster (superfine) sugar
1 egg
1 teaspoon vanilla extract
½ cup (60g) ground almonds
¾ cup (110g) plain (all-purpose) flour
¼ cup (25g) cocoa powder
¼ cup (35g) finely chopped dried cranberries
2 tablespoons jellied cranberry sauce
1 tablespoon cocoa powder, extra
CHOCOLATE GANACHE
185g (6 ounces) dark eating chocolate,
 chopped coarsely
90g (3 ounces) butter, chopped coarsely

1 Beat butter, sugar, egg and extract in small bowl with electric mixer until combined. Stir in ground almonds, sifted flour and cocoa, dried cranberries and sauce. Cover; refrigerate 1 hour.
2 Preheat oven to 180°C/350°F. Line oven trays with baking paper.
3 Roll dough between sheets of baking paper until 3mm (⅛ inch) thick. Cut 4cm (1½ inch) fluted rounds from dough; place rounds about 2.5cm (1 inch) apart on trays. Bake about 8 minutes; stand biscuits on trays 5 minutes before transferring to wire rack to cool.
4 Meanwhile, make chocolate ganache.
5 Spoon ganache into piping bag fitted with 2cm (¾ inch) fluted tube. Pipe ganache onto flat-side of half of the biscuits; top with remaining biscuits. Refrigerate until firm. Before serving, dust with a little extra sifted cocoa.
CHOCOLATE GANACHE Stir chocolate and butter in small heatproof bowl over small saucepan of simmering water until smooth; cool. Refrigerate about 20 minutes or until spreadable. Beat with electric mixer until thick and glossy.

prep + cook time 45 minutes (+ refrigeration)
makes 25

notes This dough is quite soft. If it becomes difficult to handle, roll it out, then refrigerate again until firm. Unfilled biscuits will keep in an airtight container for up to a week. Filled biscuits will keep for a few days in an airtight container in the fridge.

hazelnut moments with choc berry filling

90g (3 ounces) butter, softened
½ teaspoon vanilla extract
¼ cup (55g) caster (superfine) sugar
1 egg
½ cup (50g) ground hazelnuts
¾ cup (110g) plain (all-purpose) flour
¼ cup (25g) cocoa powder
CHOC BERRY FILLING
90g (3 ounces) dark eating chocolate, melted
60g (2 ounces) butter, softened
⅓ cup (110g) chocolate-hazelnut spread
¼ cup (35g) fresh raspberries, chopped coarsely

1 Beat butter, extract, sugar and egg in small bowl with electric mixer until combined. Stir in ground hazelnuts, then sifted flour and cocoa.
2 Divide dough in half; roll each half between sheets of baking paper until 3mm (⅛ inch) thick. Refrigerate 30 minutes.
3 Preheat oven to 180°C/350°F. Line oven trays with baking paper.
4 Cut dough into 4cm (1½ inch) fluted rounds; place on trays 2.5cm (1 inch) apart. Bake about 8 minutes. Cool on trays.
5 Make choc berry filling.
6 Spoon choc berry filling into piping bag fitted with 2cm (¾ inch) fluted tube. Pipe filling onto flat side of half the biscuits; top with remaining biscuits.
CHOC BERRY FILLING Beat cooled chocolate, butter and spread in small bowl with electric mixer until thick and glossy. Fold in raspberries.
prep + cook time 30 minutes
(+ refrigeration and cooling) **makes** 24
note Unfilled biscuits will keep in an airtight container for up to a week. Filled biscuits will keep for a few days in an airtight container in the fridge.

coconut chocolate crunchies

125g (4 ounces) butter, softened
¾ cup (165g) firmly packed light brown sugar
1 tablespoon golden syrup or treacle
2 eggs
2 cups (300g) self-raising flour
1 cup (80g) desiccated coconut
½ cup (45g) quick-cooking oats
MILK CHOCOLATE GANACHE
185g (6 ounces) milk eating chocolate,
  chopped coarsely
30g butter

1 Preheat oven to 180°C/350°F. Line oven trays with baking paper.
2 Beat butter, sugar and syrup in small bowl with electric mixer until smooth. Beat in eggs, one at a time. Stir in sifted flour, coconut and oats.

3 Roll rounded teaspoons of mixture into balls; place about 5cm (2 inches) apart on trays. Flatten with fork. Bake about 12 minutes; cool on trays.
4 Meanwhile, make milk chocolate ganache.
5 Sandwich biscuits with milk chocolate ganache; refrigerate until firm.
MILK CHOCOLATE GANACHE Stir chocolate and butter in small heatproof bowl over small saucepan of simmering water until smooth; cool.
prep + cook time 40 minutes
(+ refrigeration and cooling) **makes** 40
notes Unfilled biscuits will keep in an airtight container for up to a week. Filled biscuits will keep for a few days in an airtight container in the fridge.

wagonettes

⅓ cup (75g) caster (superfine) sugar
⅓ cup (80ml) water
2 teaspoons gelatine
⅓ cup (110g) strawberry jam (conserve),
  warmed, strained
32 (400g) milk-chocolate wheaten biscuits (see notes)
½ teaspoon vanilla extract
pink food colouring

1 Combine sugar and half the water in small
saucepan; stir over low heat until sugar dissolves.
2 Combine gelatine and the remaining water in
small jug. Pour gelatine mixture into hot sugar
syrup; stir over medium heat about 3 minutes or
until gelatine dissolves. Pour mixture into small
heatproof bowl; cool.
3 Spread jam onto the plain side of half the biscuits.

4 To make marshmallow, beat gelatine mixture in
small bowl with electric mixer on high speed for about
8 minutes or until very thick. Beat in extract and a few
drops of colouring.
5 Spoon marshmallow into piping bag fitted with
2cm (¾ inch) plain tube. Pipe marshmallow over jam;
top with remaining biscuits.
prep + cook time 30 minutes (+ cooling) **makes** 16
notes You need 2 x 200g (6½ ounce) packets
milk chocolate wheaten biscuits for this recipe.
If the marshmallow sets too quickly, return it to the
mixer bowl with about 1 tablespoon boiling water
and beat it for about a minute.
Unfilled biscuits will keep in an airtight container
for up to a week. Filled biscuits will keep for a
few days in an airtight container in the fridge.

mint slice biscuits

60g (2 ounces) butter, softened
¼ cup (55g) caster (superfine) sugar
1 egg
½ teaspoon vanilla extract
1 cup (150g) plain (all-purpose) flour
2 tablespoons cocoa powder
2 teaspoons milk, approximately
48 (350g) soft chocolate-coated mints
185g (6 ounces) dark eating chocolate, melted

1 Beat butter, sugar, egg and extract in small bowl with electric mixer until combined. Stir in sifted flour and cocoa and enough milk to make a firm dough. Cover dough; refrigerate 30 minutes.
2 Preheat oven to 180°C/350°F. Line oven trays with baking paper.
3 Roll dough between sheets of baking paper until 5mm (¼ inch) thick; cut 3.5cm (1¼ inch) rounds from dough. Place rounds about 2.5cm (1 inch) apart on trays.
4 Bake about 10 minutes; immediately place one chocolate mint on top of each biscuit, press down lightly. Cool biscuits on trays.
5 Place biscuits on wire rack over baking-paper lined tray; drizzle with chocolate. Stand at room temperature until set.
prep + cook time 45 minutes
(+ refrigeration and standing) **makes** 48
notes Unfilled biscuits will keep in an airtight container for up to a week. Filled biscuits will keep for a few days in an airtight container in the fridge.
We used individually wrapped chocolate-coated mints for this recipe. They come in a 175g (5½ ounce) box of 24 chocolates.

lemon meringue kisses

Combine 90g (3 ounces) chopped unsalted butter, 1 lightly beaten egg, ¼ cup caster (superfine) sugar, ½ teaspoon finely grated lemon rind and 2 tablespoons lemon juice in small heatproof bowl. Stir over small saucepan of simmering water about 10 minutes or until mixture coats the back of a spoon. Refrigerate lemon curd 3 hours or overnight. Preheat oven to 120°C/250°F. Grease oven trays; line with baking paper. Beat 2 egg whites, ½ cup caster (superfine) sugar and 1 teaspoon lemon juice in small bowl with electric mixer about 15 minutes or until sugar is dissolved. Spoon mixture into piping bag fitted with 2cm (¾ inch) fluted tube; pipe 4cm (1½ inch) stars onto trays 2cm (¾ inch) apart. Bake meringues about 1 hour. Cool on trays. Sandwich meringues with lemon curd; dust with sifted icing sugar if you like.
prep + cook time 1 hour 50 minutes (+ refrigeration and cooling) **makes** 24

passionfruit meringue kisses

Preheat oven to 120°C/250°F. Grease oven trays; line with baking paper. Beat 2 egg whites, ½ cup caster (superfine) sugar and a few drops of yellow food colouring in small bowl with electric mixer about 15 minutes or until sugar is dissolved. Fold in 1 teaspoon strained passionfruit juice and 1 teaspoon cornflour (cornstarch). Spoon mixture into piping bag fitted with 2cm (¾ inch) fluted tube; pipe 4cm (1½ inch) stars onto trays 2cm (¾ inch) apart. Bake about 1 hour. Cool on trays. Meanwhile, beat 60g (2 ounces) softened unsalted butter and ¾ cup sifted icing (confectioners') sugar in small bowl with electric mixer until light and fluffy. Stir in 1 tablespoon passionfruit pulp. Sandwich meringues with passionfruit butter.

prep + cook time 1 hour 25 minutes (+ cooling) **makes** 24

macaroons

chocolate almond macaroons

3 egg whites
¼ cup (55g) caster (superfine) sugar
1 cup (160g) icing (confectioners') sugar
¼ cup (25g) cocoa powder
1 cup (120g) ground almonds
2 teaspoons cocoa powder, extra
¼ cup (60ml) pouring cream
150g (5 ounces) dark eating chocolate,
  chopped finely

1 Grease oven trays; line with baking paper.
2 Beat egg whites in small bowl with electric mixer until soft peaks form. Add caster sugar, beat until sugar dissolves; transfer mixture to large bowl. Fold in sifted icing sugar and cocoa, and ground almonds, in two batches.

3 Spoon mixture into piping bag fitted with 2cm (¾ inch) plain tube. Pipe 4cm (1½ inch) rounds about 2cm (¾ inch) apart onto trays. Tap trays on bench so macaroons spread slightly. Dust macaroons with extra sifted cocoa; stand 30 minutes.
4 Meanwhile, preheat oven to 150°C/300°F.
5 Bake macaroons about 20 minutes. Cool on trays.
6 Bring cream to the boil in small saucepan, remove from heat; add chocolate, stir until smooth. Refrigerate about 20 minutes or until spreadable.
7 Sandwich macaroons with chocolate filling.
prep + cook time 40 minutes
(+ standing and refrigeration) **makes** 16
notes Unfilled macaroons will keep in an airtight container for about a week. Fill macaroons just before serving.

coconut almond macaroons

3 egg whites
¼ cup (55g) caster (superfine) sugar
½ teaspoon coconut essence
1¼ cups (200g) icing (confectioners') sugar
¾ cup (90g) ground almonds
¼ cup (20g) desiccated coconut
2 teaspoons icing (confectioners') sugar, extra
¼ cup (60ml) pouring cream
150g (5 ounces) white eating chocolate,
  chopped finely
2 teaspoons coconut-flavoured liqueur

1 Grease oven trays; line with baking paper.
2 Beat egg whites in small bowl with electric mixer until soft peaks form. Add caster sugar and essence, beat until sugar dissolves; transfer mixture to large bowl. Fold in sifted icing sugar, ground almonds and coconut, in two batches.
3 Spoon mixture into piping bag fitted with 2cm (¾ inch) plain tube. Pipe 4cm (1½ inch) rounds about 2cm (¾ inch) apart onto trays. Tap trays on bench so macaroons spread slightly. Dust macaroons with extra sifted icing sugar; stand 30 minutes.
4 Meanwhile, preheat oven to 150°C/300°F.
5 Bake macaroons about 20 minutes. Cool on trays.
6 Bring cream to the boil in small saucepan, remove from heat; add chocolate, stir until smooth. Stir in liqueur. Refrigerate 20 minutes or until spreadable.
7 Sandwich macaroons with chocolate filling.
prep + cook time 40 minutes
(+ standing and refrigeration) **makes** 16
notes Unfilled macaroons will keep in an airtight container for about a week. Fill macaroons just before serving.

orange almond macaroons

3 egg whites
¼ cup (55g) caster (superfine) sugar
orange food colouring
1¼ cups (200g) icing (confectioners') sugar
1 cup (120g) ground almonds
1 teaspoon finely grated orange rind
2 tablespoons flaked almonds
⅓ cup (115g) orange marmalade

1 Grease oven trays; line with baking paper.
2 Beat egg whites in small bowl with electric mixer until soft peaks form. Add caster sugar and a few drops of colouring, beat until sugar dissolves; transfer mixture to large bowl. Fold in sifted icing sugar, ground almonds and rind, in two batches.

3 Spoon mixture into piping bag fitted with 2cm (¾ inch) plain tube. Pipe 4cm (1½ inch) rounds about 2cm (¾ inch) apart onto trays. Tap trays on bench so macaroons spread slightly. Sprinkle macaroons with flaked almonds; stand 30 minutes.
4 Meanwhile, preheat oven to 150°C/300°F.
5 Bake macaroons about 20 minutes. Cool on trays.
6 Sandwich macaroons with marmalade.
prep + cook time 40 minutes
(+ standing and cooling) **makes** 16
notes Unfilled macaroons will keep in an airtight container for about a week. Fill macaroons just before serving. If the marmalade is too chunky or thick to spread, warm it, strain it, and leave it to cool before using.

pistachio and orange blossom macaroons

⅓ cup (45g) unsalted roasted pistachios
3 egg whites
¼ cup (55g) caster (superfine) sugar
green food colouring
1¼ cups (200g) icing (confectioners') sugar
¾ cup (90g) ground almonds
1 tablespoon icing (confectioners') sugar, extra
¼ cup (60ml) pouring cream
150g (5 ounces) white eating chocolate,
  chopped coarsely
4 teaspoons orange blossom water

1 Grease oven trays; line with baking paper.
2 Process pistachios until ground finely.
3 Beat egg whites in small bowl with electric mixer until soft peaks form. Add caster sugar and a few drops of colouring, beat until sugar dissolves; transfer mixture to large bowl. Fold in ¼ cup of the ground pistachios, sifted icing sugar and ground almonds, in two batches.
4 Spoon mixture into piping bag fitted with 2cm (¾ inch) plain tube. Pipe 4cm (1½ inch) rounds about 2cm (¾ inch) apart onto trays. Tap trays on bench so macaroons spread slightly. Dust macaroons with extra sifted icing sugar; sprinkle with remaining ground pistachios. Stand 30 minutes.
5 Meanwhile, preheat oven to 150°C/300°F.
6 Bake macaroons about 20 minutes. Cool on trays.
7 Bring cream to the boil in small saucepan, remove from heat; add chocolate, stir until smooth. Stir in orange blossom water. Refrigerate until spreadable.
8 Sandwich macaroons with chocolate filling.
prep + cook time 40 minutes
(+ standing and refrigeration) **makes** 16
notes Unfilled macaroons will keep in an airtight container for about a week. Fill macaroons just before serving.

lemon liqueur macaroons

3 egg whites
¼ cup (55g) caster (superfine) sugar
yellow food colouring
1¼ cups (200g) icing (confectioners') sugar
1 cup (120g) ground almonds
2 teaspoons finely grated lemon rind
1 tablespoon icing (confectioners') sugar, extra
¼ cup (60ml) pouring cream
150g (5 ounces) white chocolate,
   chopped coarsely
4 teaspoons limoncello liqueur

1 Grease oven trays; line with baking paper.
2 Beat egg whites in small bowl with electric mixer until soft peaks form. Add caster sugar and a few drops of colouring, beat until sugar dissolves; transfer mixture to large bowl. Fold in sifted icing sugar, ground almonds and rind, in two batches.
3 Spoon mixture into piping bag fitted with 2cm (¾ inch) plain tube. Pipe 4cm (1½ inch) rounds about 2cm (¾ inch) apart onto trays. Tap trays on bench so macaroons spread slightly. Dust macaroons with extra sifted icing sugar. Stand 30 minutes.
4 Meanwhile, preheat oven to 150°C/300°F.
5 Bake macaroons about 20 minutes. Cool on trays.
6 Bring cream to the boil in small saucepan, remove from heat; add chocolate, stir until smooth. Stir in liqueur, stand at room temperature until spreadable.
7 Sandwich macaroons with chocolate filling.
prep + cook time 40 minutes (+ standing) **makes** 16
notes Unfilled macaroons will keep in an airtight container for about a week. Fill macaroons just before serving.

coconut macaroons

2 egg whites
½ cup (110g) caster (superfine) sugar
1 teaspoon vanilla extract
¼ cup (35g) plain (all-purpose) flour
1½ cups (120g) desiccated coconut
6 glacé cherries, quartered

1 Preheat oven to 150°C/300°F. Grease oven trays; line with baking paper.
2 Beat egg whites in small bowl with electric mixer until soft peaks form. Gradually add sugar, beating until dissolved between additions. Stir in extract, sifted flour and coconut, in two batches.
3 Drop level tablespoons of the mixture onto trays about 5cm (2 inches) apart. Place cherry quarter on top of each macaroon. Bake about 30 minutes. Cool on trays.

prep + cook time 50 minutes **makes** 24
notes Macaroons will keep in an airtight container for about a week.
Glacé cherries are available in three colours, if they're hard to find use any type of glacé fruit you like.

coconut, cranberry and white chocolate macaroons

2 egg whites
½ cup (110g) caster (superfine) sugar
1 teaspoon vanilla extract
¼ cup (35g) plain (all-purpose) flour
1½ cups (120g) desiccated coconut
⅓ cup (45g) dried cranberries, chopped coarsely
90g (3 ounces) white eating chocolate, chopped finely
28 whole dried cranberries

1 Preheat oven to 150°C/300°F. Grease oven trays; line with baking paper.
2 Beat egg whites in small bowl with electric mixer until soft peaks form. Gradually add sugar, beating until dissolved after each addition. Stir in extract, sifted flour, coconut, chopped cranberries and chocolate, in two batches.
3 Using wet hands, roll rounded tablespoons of mixture into balls; place about 5cm (2 inches) apart onto trays. Press a whole cranberry on each macaroon. Bake macaroons about 25 minutes; cool on trays.
prep + cook time 50 minutes **makes** 28
note Macaroons will keep in an airtight container for about a week.

63

dark chocolate and walnut macaroons

2 cups (200g) walnuts
2 egg whites
½ cup (110g) caster (superfine) sugar
1 teaspoon vanilla extract
1 tablespoon plain (all-purpose) flour
4 teaspoons cocoa powder
90g (3 ounces) dark eating chocolate, chopped finely
60g (2 ounces) dark eating chocolate, melted

1 Preheat oven to 150°C/300°F. Grease oven trays; line with baking paper.
2 Blend or process walnuts until ground finely.
3 Beat egg whites in small bowl with electric mixer until soft peaks form. Gradually add sugar, beating until dissolved after each addition. Stir in extract, sifted flour and cocoa, ground walnuts and chopped chocolate, in two batches.
4 Drop rounded tablespoons of mixture 5cm (2 inches) apart onto trays. Bake macaroons about 25 minutes; cool on trays.
5 Drizzle cooled macaroons with melted chocolate; stand at room temperature until set.
prep + cook time 1 hour (+ standing) **makes** 24
note Macaroons will keep in an airtight container for about a week.

caramel pecan macaroons

1⅔ cups (200g) pecans
2 egg whites
½ cup (110g) firmly packed light brown sugar
1 teaspoon vanilla extract
¼ cup (35g) plain (all-purpose) flour
22 pecan halves

1 Preheat oven to 150°C/300°F. Grease oven trays; line with baking paper.
2 Blend or process pecans until ground finely.
3 Beat egg whites and sugar in small bowl with electric mixer about 15 minutes or until sugar is dissolved. Stir in extract, sifted flour and ground pecans, in two batches.
4 Drop rounded tablespoons of mixture 5cm (2 inches) apart onto trays. Press one nut on top of each macaroon. Bake about 30 minutes; cool on trays.

prep + cook time 55 minutes **makes** 22
note Macaroons will keep in an airtight container for about a week.

honey almond macaroons

2 egg whites
½ cup (110g) caster (superfine) sugar
1 teaspoon vanilla extract
4 teaspoons honey
¼ cup (35g) plain (all-purpose) flour
1 cup (120g) ground almonds
1 cup (80g) desiccated coconut
¼ cup (20g) flaked almonds
1 tablespoon icing (confectioners') sugar

1 Preheat oven to 150°C/300°F. Grease oven trays; line with baking paper.
2 Beat egg whites in small bowl with electric mixer until soft peaks form. Gradually add caster sugar, beating until dissolved after each addition. Stir in extract, honey, sifted flour, ground almonds and coconut, in two batches.
3 Drop level tablespoons of mixture about 5cm (2 inches) apart onto trays. Sprinkle macaroons with flaked almonds. Bake about 45 minutes; cool on trays.
4 Dust macaroons with sifted icing sugar.
prep + cook time 55 minutes **makes** 26
note Macaroons will keep in an airtight container for about a week.

almond macaroons

2 egg whites
½ cup (110g) caster (superfine) sugar
1¼ cups (125g) ground almonds
½ teaspoon almond extract
¼ cup (35g) plain (all-purpose) flour
18 whole blanched almonds

1 Preheat oven to 150°C/300°F. Grease oven trays; line with baking paper.
2 Beat egg whites in small bowl with electric mixer until soft peaks form. Gradually add sugar, beating until dissolved between additions. Fold in ground almonds, extract and sifted flour, in two batches.
3 Drop level tablespoons of mixture about 5cm (2 inches) apart onto trays. Place one blanched almond on top of each macaroon. Bake about 1 hour. Cool on trays.

prep + cook time 1 hour 20 minutes **makes** 18
note Macaroons will keep in an airtight container for about a week.

raspberry macaroon dreams

3 egg whites
¼ cup (55g) caster (superfine) sugar
pink food colouring
1¼ cups (240g) icing (confectioners') sugar
1 cup (120g) ground almonds
1 tablespoon raspberry purée (see notes)
1 tablespoon icing (confectioners') sugar, extra
¼ cup (60ml) pouring cream
150g (5 ounces) white eating chocolate,
  chopped coarsely
1 tablespoon raspberry jam (conserve),
  warmed, sieved

1 Grease oven trays; line with baking paper.
2 Beat egg whites in small bowl with electric mixer until soft peaks form. Add caster sugar and a few drops of colouring, beat until sugar dissolves; transfer mixture to large bowl. Fold in sifted icing sugar, ground almonds and raspberry purée, in two batches.
3 Spoon mixture into piping bag fitted with 2cm (¾ inch) plain tube. Pipe 4cm (1½ inch) rounds about 2cm (¾ inch) apart onto trays. Tap trays on bench so macaroons spread slightly. Dust macaroons with extra sifted icing sugar; stand 30 minutes.
4 Meanwhile, preheat oven to 150°C/300°F.
5 Bake macaroons about 20 minutes. Cool on trays.
6 Bring cream to the boil in small saucepan, remove from heat; add chocolate, stir until smooth. Stir in jam and tint with colouring. Refrigerate until spreadable.
7 Sandwich macaroons with chocolate filling.
prep + cook time 40 minutes
(+ standing and refrigeration) **makes** 16
notes Push 6 fresh or thawed frozen raspberries through a fine sieve to make raspberry purée. Unfilled macaroons will keep in an airtight container for about a week. Fill macaroons just before serving.

biscotti

almond bread

3 egg whites
½ cup (110g) caster (superfine) sugar
1 cup (150g) plain (all-purpose) flour
¾ cup (120g) almond kernels

1 Preheat oven to 180°C/350°F. Grease 10cm x 20cm (4 inch x 8 inch) loaf pan.
2 Beat egg whites in small bowl with electric mixer until soft peaks form. Gradually add sugar, beating until dissolved between additions.
3 Fold sifted flour and nuts into egg white mixture, spread mixture into pan; bake about 30 minutes. Cool bread in pan. Remove bread from pan, wrap in foil; stand overnight.

4 Preheat oven to 150°C/300°F.
5 Using a sharp serrated knife, cut the bread into wafer-thin slices. Place slices, in single layer, on ungreased oven trays. Bake about 45 minutes or until dry and crisp.

prep + cook time 1 hour 35 minutes (+ cooling and standing) **makes** 40
notes Almond bread is an excellent accompaniment to desserts such as mousse, sorbet or ice-cream. It will keep for months if stored in an airtight container.

jaffa biscotti

1 cup (220g) caster (superfine) sugar
2 eggs
1⅓ cups (200g) plain (all-purpose) flour
⅓ cup (50g) self-raising flour
¼ cup (25g) cocoa powder
¾ cup (165g) finely chopped glacé orange

1 Preheat oven to 180°C/350°F. Grease oven tray.
2 Whisk sugar and eggs in medium bowl until combined; stir in sifted flours and cocoa then orange.
3 Knead dough on floured surface until smooth. Divide dough in half, roll each portion into a 30cm (12 inch) log; place logs on tray. Bake about 30 minutes. Cool on tray 10 minutes.

4 Reduce oven temperature to 150°C/300°F.
5 Using serrated knife, cut logs diagonally into 5mm (¼ inch) slices. Place slices, in single layer, on ungreased oven trays. Bake biscotti about 30 minutes or until dry and crisp, turning halfway through baking. Cool on wire racks.
prep + cook time 1 hour 25 minutes **makes** 60
notes You will need about 8 slices glacé orange for this recipe. Biscotti will keep in an airtight container for at least a month.

stained glass biscotti

¾ cup (165g) caster (superfine) sugar
2 eggs
1⅓ cups (200g) plain (all-purpose) flour
⅓ cup (50g) self-raising flour
1½ cups (300g) multi glacé cherries, halved
  (see notes)
½ cup (80g) blanched almonds

1 Preheat oven to 180°C/350°F. Grease oven tray.
2 Whisk sugar and eggs in medium bowl until combined; stir in sifted flours then cherries and nuts.
3 Knead dough on floured surface until smooth. Divide dough in half, roll each portion into a 30cm (12 inch) log; place logs on tray. Bake about 30 minutes. Cool on tray 10 minutes.

4 Reduce oven temperature to 150°C/300°F.
5 Using serrated knife, cut logs diagonally into 5mm (¼ inch) slices. Place slices, in single layer, on ungreased oven trays. Bake biscotti about 30 minutes or until dry and crisp, turning halfway through baking. Cool on wire racks.

prep + cook time 1 hour 25 minutes **makes** 60
notes Multi glacé cherries are simply a mix of red, green and yellow cherries. Biscotti will keep in an airtight container for at least a month.

citrus coconut biscotti

1 cup (220g) caster (superfine) sugar
2 eggs
1⅓ cups (200g) plain (all-purpose) flour
⅓ cup (50g) self-raising flour
1 cup (80g) desiccated coconut
2 teaspoons each finely grated lemon, lime
   and orange rind

1 Preheat oven to 180°C/350°F. Grease oven tray.
2 Whisk sugar and eggs in medium bowl until combined; stir in sifted flours then coconut and rinds.
3 Knead dough on floured surface until smooth. Divide dough in half, roll each portion into a 30cm (12 inch) log; place logs on tray. Bake about 30 minutes. Cool on tray 10 minutes.
4 Reduce oven temperature to 150°C/300°F.
5 Using serrated knife, cut logs diagonally into 5mm (¼ inch) slices. Place slices, in single layer, on ungreased oven trays. Bake biscotti about 30 minutes or until dry and crisp, turning halfway through baking. Cool on wire racks.

prep + cook time 1 hour 25 minutes   **makes** 60
note Biscotti will keep in an airtight container for at least a month.

apple, cranberry and white chocolate biscotti

1 cup (220g) caster (superfine) sugar
2 eggs
1⅓ cups (200g) plain (all-purpose) flour
⅓ cup (50g) self-raising flour
½ cup (35g) finely chopped dried apple
½ cup (65g) coarsely chopped dried cranberries
90g (3 ounces) white eating chocolate,
  grated coarsely

1 Preheat oven to 180°C/350°F. Grease oven tray.
2 Whisk sugar and eggs in medium bowl until combined; stir in sifted flours then apple, cranberries and chocolate.
3 Knead dough on floured surface until smooth. Divide dough in half, roll each portion into a 30cm (12 inch) log; place logs on tray. Bake about 30 minutes. Cool on tray 10 minutes.
4 Reduce oven temperature to 150°C/300°F.
5 Using serrated knife, cut logs diagonally into 5mm (¼ inch) slices. Place slices, in single layer, on ungreased oven trays. Bake biscotti about 30 minutes or until dry and crisp, turning halfway through baking. Cool on wire racks.
prep + cook time 1 hour 25 minutes **makes** 60
note Biscotti will keep in an airtight container for at least a month.

rosy apricot and pistachio biscotti

1 cup (220g) caster (superfine) sugar
2 eggs
1⅓ cups (200g) plain (all-purpose) flour
⅓ cup (50g) self-raising flour
⅓ cup (55g) finely chopped dried apricots
⅓ cup (45g) unsalted roasted pistachios
4 teaspoons rosewater

1 Preheat oven to 180°C/350°F. Grease oven tray.
2 Whisk sugar and eggs in medium bowl until combined; stir in sifted flours then apricots, nuts and rosewater.
3 Knead dough on floured surface until smooth. Divide dough in half, roll each portion into a 20cm (8 inch) log; place logs on tray. Bake about 30 minutes. Cool on tray 10 minutes.
4 Reduce oven temperature to 150°C/300°F.
5 Using serrated knife, cut logs diagonally into 5mm (¼ inch) slices. Place slices, in single layer, on ungreased oven trays. Bake biscotti about 30 minutes or until dry and crisp, turning halfway through baking. Cool on wire racks.
prep + cook time 1 hour 25 minutes **makes** 40
note Biscotti will keep in an airtight container for at least a month.

coffee and walnut biscotti

½ cup (110g) caster (superfine) sugar
1 egg
½ cup (75g) plain (all-purpose) flour
¼ cup (35g) self-raising flour
4 teaspoons instant coffee granules
1 cup (100g) walnuts, chopped coarsely
90g (3 ounces) dark eating chocolate, melted

1 Preheat oven to 180°C/350°F. Grease oven tray.
2 Whisk sugar and egg in medium bowl until combined; stir in sifted flours, then coffee granules and walnuts. Shape dough into a 20cm (8 inch) log; place on tray. Bake about 30 minutes. Cool on tray.
3 Reduce oven temperature to 150°C/300°F.

4 Using serrated knife, cut log diagonally into 1cm (½ inch) slices. Place slices, in single layer, on ungreased oven trays. Bake biscotti about 30 minutes or until dry and crisp, turning halfway through baking. Cool on wire racks.
5 Spread chocolate over one side of each biscotti; stand at room temperature until set.
prep + cook time 1 hour 10 minutes (+ standing)
makes 20
note Biscotti will keep in an airtight container for at least a month.

triple chocolate biscotti with hazelnuts

30g (1 ounce) butter, softened
½ cup (110g) firmly packed light brown sugar
1 teaspoon vanilla extract
3 eggs
¾ cup (110g) plain (all-purpose) flour
¼ cup (35g) self-raising flour
⅓ cup (35g) cocoa powder
1 cup (140g) roasted hazelnuts, chopped coarsely
60g (2 ounces) dark eating chocolate, chopped finely
30g (1 ounce) milk eating chocolate, chopped finely
60g (2 ounces) white eating chocolate, chopped finely

1 Beat butter, sugar and extract in small bowl with electric mixer until combined. Add eggs, beat until combined (mixture will curdle at this stage, but will come together later). Stir in sifted dry ingredients, then nuts and chocolates. Cover mixture, refrigerate 1 hour.
2 Preheat oven to 180°C/350°F. Grease oven trays.
3 Divide dough in half, roll each portion into a 15cm (6 inch) log; place logs on tray. Bake about 25 minutes. Cool on trays.
4 Reduce oven temperature to 150°C/300°F.
5 Using serrated knife, cut logs diagonally into 1cm (½ inch) slices. Place slices, in single layer, on ungreased oven trays. Bake biscotti about 30 minutes or until dry and crisp, turning halfway through baking. Cool on wire racks.
prep + cook time 1 hour 10 minutes (+ refrigeration)
makes 30
note Biscotti will keep in an airtight container for at least a month.

lemon, honey and pistachio biscotti

½ cup (110g) caster (superfine) sugar
1 egg
½ cup (75g) plain (all-purpose) flour
¼ cup (35g) self-raising flour
2 teaspoons finely grated lemon rind
½ cup (70g) unsalted roasted pistachio nuts
¼ cup (50g) pumpkin seed kernels
¼ cup (35g) sunflower seed kernels
1 tablespoon honey
2 teaspoons caster (superfine) sugar, extra

1 Preheat oven to 180°C/350°F. Grease oven tray.
2 Whisk sugar and egg in medium bowl; stir in sifted flours and rind, then nuts, seeds and honey. Shape dough into a 20cm (8 inch) log; place on tray. Sprinkle with extra sugar, bake about 30 minutes. Cool on tray.
3 Reduce oven temperature to 150°C/300°F.
4 Using serrated knife, cut log diagonally into 5mm (¼ inch) slices. Place slices, in single layer, on ungreased oven trays. Bake biscotti about 20 minutes or until dry and crisp, turning halfway through baking. Cool on wire racks.
prep + cook time 1 hour 10 minutes **makes** 40
note Biscotti will keep in an airtight container for at least a month.

gingerbread biscotti

½ cup (110g) firmly packed dark brown sugar
1 egg
½ cup (75g) plain (all-purpose) flour
¼ cup (35g) self-raising flour
4 teaspoons ground ginger
1 teaspoon ground cinnamon
¼ teaspoon ground cloves
½ cup (115g) coarsely chopped glacé ginger
LEMON GLACÉ ICING
1 cup (160g) icing (confectioners') sugar
½ teaspoon finely grated lemon rind
¼ cup (60ml) lemon juice

1 Preheat oven to 180°C/350°F. Grease oven tray.
2 Whisk sugar and egg in medium bowl until combined; stir in sifted dry ingredients, then glacé ginger. Shape dough into a 20cm (8 inch) log; place on tray, bake about 30 minutes. Cool on tray.

3 Reduce oven temperature to 150°C/300°F.
4 Using serrated knife, cut log diagonally into 5mm (¼ inch) slices. Place slices, in single layer, on ungreased oven trays. Bake biscotti about 30 minutes, turning halfway through baking. Cool on wire racks.
5 Meanwhile, make lemon glacé icing.
6 Dip one end of each biscotti into icing, place on foil-lined tray; stand at room temperature until set.
lemon glacé icing Stir sifted icing sugar, rind and juice in small bowl until smooth.

prep + cook time 1 hour 10 minutes (+ standing)
makes 40
note Biscotti will keep in an airtight container for at least a month.

slices

chocolate caramel slice

½ cup (75g) self-raising flour
½ cup (75g) plain (all-purpose) flour
1 cup (80g) desiccated coconut
1 cup (220g) firmly packed light brown sugar
125g (4 ounces) butter, melted
395g (14 ounces) canned
 sweetened condensed milk
30g (1 ounce) butter, extra
2 tablespoons golden syrup or treacle
185g (6 ounces) dark eating (semi-sweet) chocolate,
 chopped coarsely
2 teaspoons vegetable oil

1 Preheat oven to 180°C/350°F. Grease 20cm x 30cm (8 inch x 12 inch) rectangular pan; line base and long sides with baking paper, extending paper 5cm (2 inches) over sides.
2 Combine sifted flours, coconut, sugar and butter in medium bowl; press mixture evenly over base of pan. Bake about 15 minutes or until browned lightly.
3 Meanwhile, make caramel filling by combining condensed milk, extra butter and syrup in small saucepan. Stir over medium heat about 15 minutes or until caramel mixture is golden brown; pour over base. Bake 10 minutes; cool.
4 Make topping by combining chocolate and oil in small saucepan; stir over low heat until smooth. Pour warm topping over cold caramel. Refrigerate 3 hours or overnight.
prep + cook time 45 minutes
(+ cooling and refrigeration) **makes** 24
note The slice will keep in an airtight container in the fridge for up to four days.

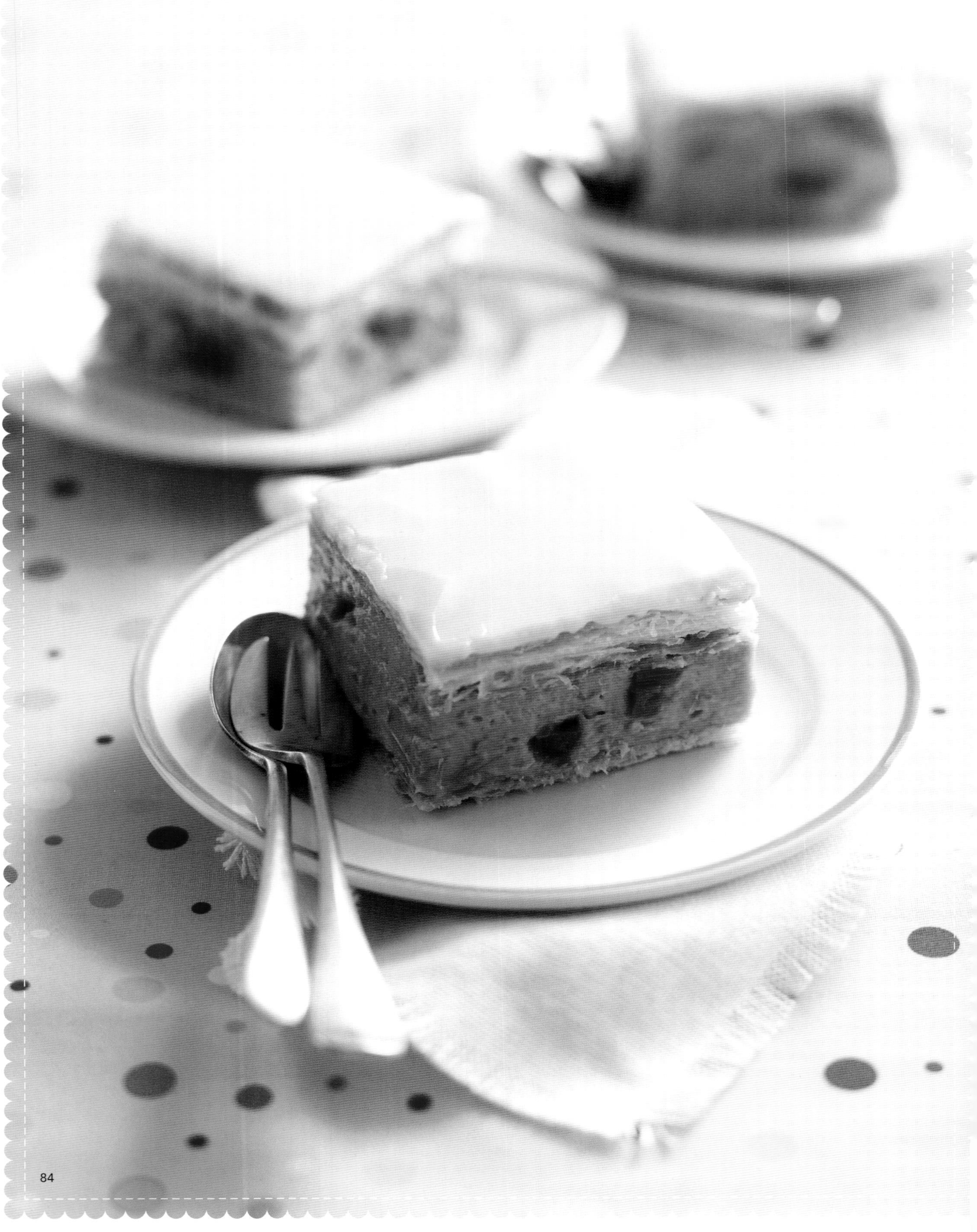

rhubarb custard slice

2 sheets ready-rolled puff pastry, thawed
4 cups (440g) coarsely chopped fresh rhubarb
⅓ cup (75g) caster (superfine) sugar
⅓ cup (80ml) water
½ cup (110g) caster (superfine) sugar, extra
½ cup (75g) cornflour (cornstarch)
¼ cup (30g) custard powder
2½ cups (625ml) milk
30g (1 ounce) butter
1 egg yolk
1 teaspoon vanilla extract
¾ cup (180ml) pouring cream
pink food colouring
ORANGE ICING
1½ cups (240g) icing (confectioners') sugar
2 tablespoons orange juice, approximately

1 Preheat oven to 220°C/425°F. Grease deep 23cm (9 inch) square cake pan; line base and sides with foil, extending foil 10cm (4 inches) over sides.
2 Place pastry sheets on separate greased oven trays. Bake about 15 minutes; cool. Flatten pastry with hand; place one pastry sheet in pan, trim to fit, if necessary.
3 Meanwhile, combine rhubarb, sugar and the water in large saucepan; cook, covered, stirring occasionally, until rhubarb mixture is pulpy. Cool.
4 Combine extra sugar, cornflour and custard powder in medium saucepan; gradually stir in milk until smooth. Add butter; stir over heat until mixture boils and thickens. Reduce heat; simmer, stirring, about 5 minutes or until custard is thick and smooth. Remove from heat; stir in egg yolk, extract, cream and rhubarb. Tint custard with pink food colouring. Spread warm custard mixture over pastry in pan. Top with remaining pastry, puffed-side down, trim to fit if necessary; press down lightly.
5 Make orange icing.
6 Spread pastry with icing; refrigerate slice 3 hours or overnight.

ORANGE ICING Sift icing sugar into small heatproof bowl; stir in enough of the juice to make a firm paste. Stir icing over small saucepan of simmering water until spreadable.

prep + cook time 45 minutes (+ refrigeration)
makes 16
notes You need about 1 large bunch of rhubarb. The slice will keep in an airtight container in the fridge for up to three days.

fruity choc chip slice

⅓ cup (75g) firmly packed light brown sugar
90g (3 ounces) butter, chopped coarsely
1¼ cups (185g) plain (all-purpose) flour
1 egg yolk
FRUITY CHOC TOPPING
2 eggs
1 cup (220g) firmly packed light brown sugar
⅓ cup (50g) self-raising flour
1 cup (190g) milk Choc Bits
1 cup (90g) rolled oats
½ cup (40g) shredded coconut
⅓ cup (45g) coarsely chopped, unsalted,
   roasted pistachios
½ cup (80g) finely chopped dried mixed berries
½ cup (30g) finely chopped dried apple

1 Preheat oven to 180°C/350°F. Grease 20cm x 30cm (8 inch x 12 inch) rectangular pan; line base and long sides with baking paper, extending paper 5cm (2 inches) over sides.
2 Stir sugar and butter in medium saucepan over low heat until smooth. Remove from heat; stir in sifted flour then egg yolk. Press mixture firmly over base of pan; bake about 10 minutes or until browned lightly. Cool.
3 Meanwhile, make fruity choc topping.
4 Spread topping over base; bake about 25 minutes or until browned lightly. Cool in pan.
FRUITY CHOC TOPPING Beat eggs and sugar in small bowl with electric mixer until thick and pale, transfer to large bowl; fold in sifted flour then remaining ingredients.
prep + cook time 1 hour **makes** 24
note Slice can be stored in an airtight container for up to a week.

blueberry macaroon slice

90g (3 ounces) butter, softened
½ cup (110g) caster (superfine) sugar
1 egg
⅔ cup (100g) plain (all-purpose) flour
¼ cup (35g) self-raising flour
1 tablespoon custard powder
½ cup (160g) blueberry jam (conserve)
COCONUT TOPPING
2 egg whites, beaten lightly
2½ cups (190g) shredded coconut
¼ cup (55g) caster (superfine) sugar

1 Preheat oven to 180°C/350°F. Grease 20cm x 30cm (8 inch x 12 inch) rectangular pan; line base and long sides with baking paper, extending paper 5cm (2 inches) over sides.
2 Beat butter, sugar and egg in small bowl with electric mixer until combined; stir in sifted flours and custard powder. Spread dough into pan; spread with jam.
3 Make coconut topping; sprinkle over jam.
4 Bake slice about 40 minutes; cool in pan.
COCONUT TOPPING Place ingredients in medium bowl; stir to combine.
prep + cook time 1 hour **makes** 32
note Slice can be stored in an airtight container for up to a week.

rich chocolate hazelnut slice

250g (8 ounces) plain chocolate biscuits
¾ cup (110g) roasted hazelnuts, coarsely chopped
155g (5 ounces) unsalted butter, melted
395g (14 ounces) canned sweetened
   condensed milk
375g (12 ounces) milk eating chocolate,
   chopped coarsely
315g (10 ounces) dark eating (semi-sweet)
   chocolate, chopped coarsely
15g (½ ounce) unsalted butter, extra
30g (1 ounce) white eating chocolate, melted

1 Grease 20cm x 30cm (8 inch x 12 inch) rectangular pan; line base and long sides with baking paper, extending paper 5cm (2 inches) over sides.
2 Process biscuits and ¼ cup of the nuts until fine; add butter, process until combined. Press mixture over base of pan. Refrigerate about 20 minutes or until firm.
3 Combine condensed milk and 345g (11 ounces) of the milk chocolate in small saucepan; stir over low heat until smooth. Stir in remaining nuts. Working quickly, spread chocolate mixture over base.
4 Combine dark chocolate and extra butter in small saucepan; stir over low heat until smooth. Spread over milk chocolate layer.
5 Melt remaining milk chocolate; drizzle milk and white chocolate over slice. Refrigerate 20 minutes or until firm.
prep + cook time 30 minutes (+ refrigeration)
makes 32
note Slice will keep in an airtight container in the fridge for up to a week.

raspberry coconut slice

90g (3 ounces) butter, softened
½ cup (110g) caster (superfine) sugar
1 egg
¼ cup (35g) self-raising flour
⅔ cup (100g) plain (all-purpose) flour
1 tablespoon custard powder
⅔ cup (220g) raspberry jam (conserve)
COCONUT TOPPING
2 cups (160g) desiccated coconut
¼ cup (55g) caster (superfine) sugar
2 eggs, beaten lightly

1 Preheat oven to 180°C/350°F. Grease 20cm x 30cm (8 inch x 12 inch) rectangular pan; line base and long sides with baking paper, extending paper 5cm (2 inches) over sides.
2 Beat butter, sugar and egg in small bowl with electric mixer until light and fluffy. Transfer to medium bowl; stir in sifted flours and custard powder. Spread dough into pan; spread with jam.
3 Make coconut topping; sprinkle over jam.
4 Bake slice about 40 minutes; cool in pan.
COCONUT TOPPING Place ingredients in medium bowl; stir to combine.
prep + cook time 1 hour **makes** 16
note Slice can be stored in an airtight container for up to a week.

pear and raspberry streusel slice

3 medium pears (700g), peeled, cored,
   sliced thinly
¼ cup (55g) caster (superfine) sugar
¼ cup (60ml) water
90g (3 ounces) butter, softened
⅓ cup (75g) caster (superfine) sugar, extra
1 egg
1 cup (150g) self-raising flour
⅓ cup (80ml) milk
155g (5 ounces) fresh or frozen raspberries
¼ cup (30g) finely chopped walnuts
STREUSEL TOPPING
⅓ cup (50g) plain (all-purpose) flour
2 tablespoons self-raising flour
¼ cup (55g) firmly packed light brown sugar
1 teaspoon mixed spice
90g (3 ounces) cold butter, chopped coarsely

1 Make streusel topping.
2 Preheat oven to 180°C/350°F. Grease 20cm x 30cm
(8 inch x 12 inch) rectangular pan; line base and
long sides with baking paper, extending paper
5cm (2 inches) over sides.

3 Combine pear, sugar and the water in large
saucepan; cook, covered, stirring occasionally, about
10 minutes or until pear softens. Drain, then cool.
4 Beat butter and extra sugar in small bowl with
electric mixer until light and fluffy. Add egg; beat until
combined. Stir in sifted flour and milk, in two batches.
Spread mixture into pan; bake 15 minutes. Remove
from oven.
5 Increase oven temperature to 200°C/400°F.
6 Working quickly, arrange pear over base; sprinkle
with raspberries and nuts. Coarsely grate streusel
over fruit mixture. Bake slice about 20 minutes. Stand
slice in pan 10 minutes before turning, top-side-up,
onto wire rack to cool.
7 Serve slice warm or cold.
STREUSEL TOPPING Process ingredients until
combined. Wrap in plastic; freeze 1 hour or until firm.
prep + cook time 1 hour 10 minutes
(+ freezing and cooling) **makes** 12
notes This recipe is best served warm and would be
delicious as a dessert with ice-cream.
Slice will keep in an airtight container in the fridge
for two days.

turkish delight slice

185g (6 ounces) unsalted butter, softened
⅓ cup (75g) caster (superfine) sugar
1 teaspoon vanilla extract
1½ cups (225g) plain (all-purpose) flour
⅓ cup (50g) self-raising flour
4 teaspoons gelatine
2 tablespoons water
⅓ cup (80ml) water, extra
1½ cups (330g) white (granulated) sugar
⅓ cup (50g) cornflour (cornstarch)
2 tablespoons rosewater
red food colouring
2 tablespoons icing (confectioners') sugar

1 Preheat oven to 180°C/350°F. Grease 20cm x 30cm (8 inch x 12 inch) rectangular pan; line base and long sides with baking paper, extending paper 5cm (2 inches) over sides.
2 Beat butter, caster sugar and extract in small bowl with electric mixer until combined. Stir in sifted flours. Press mixture evenly over base of pan; using fork, rough the surface. Bake base about 20 minutes or until golden brown. Cool.

3 Sprinkle gelatine over the water in small heatproof jug; stand jug in small saucepan of simmering water, stir until gelatine dissolves.
4 Reserve 1 tablespoon of the extra water. Stir the remaining extra water and white sugar in medium saucepan over low heat, without boiling, until sugar dissolves; bring to the boil. Boil, uncovered, without stirring, until temperature reaches 116°C (240°F) on a candy thermometer. Reduce heat; simmer, uncovered, 5 minutes, without stirring, regulating heat to maintain temperature at 116°C (240°F). Remove from heat.
5 Blend cornflour with the reserved 1 tablespoon water, gelatine mixture, rosewater and a few drops of food colouring until smooth; stir into sugar syrup. Return to heat; simmer, stirring, about 3 minutes or until mixture is opaque. Strain mixture over slice base, skim any scum from surface; stand 3 hours or overnight at room temperature.
6 Sprinkle slice with sifted icing sugar to serve.
prep + cook time 1 hour (+ standing) **makes** 24
notes It's important to use a candy thermometer for guaranteed success with this recipe.
Slice can be stored, refrigerated in an airtight container, for up to 4 days. Use a hot wet knife to cut the slice.

chocolate peanut slice

1½ sheets ready-rolled shortcrust pastry
⅔ cup (220g) raspberry jam (conserve)
3 egg whites
1½ cups (330g) caster (superfine) sugar
1 cup (110g) plain cake crumbs
⅓ cup (35g) cocoa powder
1 teaspoon vanilla extract
1¾ cups (250g) roasted unsalted peanuts
2 teaspoons icing sugar

1 Preheat oven to 200°C/400°F.
2 Place pastry pieces on flat oven tray, prick all over with a fork; bake about 10 minutes or until pastry is browned lightly and almost cooked through. Place hot pastry pieces, side-by-side, on flat surface; using base of a 20cm x 30cm (8 inch x 12 inch) rectangular pan as a guide, cut pastry to fit pan. Grease and line base and sides of pan; place cut pastry pieces into base of pan, spread evenly with jam.
3 Reduce oven temperature to 180°C/350°F.
4 Beat egg whites in small bowl with electric mixer until firm peaks form. Beat in sugar in three batches (see notes). Stir in cake crumbs, sifted cocoa, extract then nuts. Spread nut mixture evenly over jam.
5 Bake slice about 40 minutes. Cool in pan before cutting. Dust with sifted icing sugar before serving.
prep + cook time 1 hour (+ cooling) **makes** 30
notes When beating sugar into the egg white, beat only until combined; the sugar will not dissolve at this stage. Slice can be stored in an airtight container in the fridge for a week.

choc-caramel slice

2 packets original Tim Tam chocolate biscuits
(see notes)
45g (1½ ounces) unsalted butter, chopped
⅓ cup (80ml) sweetened condensed milk
185g (6 ounces) jersey caramels,
chopped coarsely
CHOCOLATE TOPPING
250g (8 ounces) milk eating chocolate,
chopped coarsely
2 teaspoons vegetable oil

1 Grease 20cm x 30cm (8 inch x 12 inch) rectangular
pan; line base and long sides with baking paper,
extending paper 5cm (2 inches) over sides.
2 Process half the biscuits until fine. Chop remaining
biscuits coarsely.

3 Combine butter and condensed milk in small
saucepan; stir over low heat until smooth.
4 Combine processed and chopped biscuits with
caramels in medium bowl; stir in butter mixture. Press
mixture firmly into pan. Refrigerate 30 minutes.
5 Meanwhile, make chocolate topping.
6 Spread chocolate topping over slice. Refrigerate
about 30 minutes or until firm.
CHOCOLATE TOPPING Stir ingredients in small
heatproof bowl over small saucepan of simmering
water until smooth.
prep + cook time 30 minutes (+ refrigeration)
makes 20
notes You need to buy 2 x 200g (6½ ounce) packets
of Tim Tams for this recipe. The slice will keep in an
airtight container in the fridge for up to four days.

chocolate brownie slice >

Preheat oven to 180°C/350°F. Grease deep 20cm (8 inch) square cake pan; line base with baking paper, extending paper 5cm (2 inches) over sides. Combine 125g (4 ounces) chopped butter and 185g (6 ounces) chopped dark eating chocolate in medium saucepan; stir over low heat until smooth. Cool 10 minutes. Stir in ½ cup caster (superfine) sugar and 2 eggs then 1¼ cups sifted plain (all-purpose) flour, 155g (5 ounces) chopped white eating chocolate and 90g (3 ounces) chopped milk eating chocolate. Spread mixture into pan. Bake about 35 minutes. Cool in pan.

prep + cook time 1 hour **makes** 25

< chocky nut and cornflake slice

Grease 20cm x 30cm (8 inch x 12 inch) rectangular pan; line base and long sides with baking paper, extending paper 5cm (2 inches) over sides. Stir 125g (4 ounces) coarsely chopped butter, ½ cup caster (superfine) sugar, ⅓ cup light corn syrup and ⅓ cup crunchy peanut butter in large saucepan over low heat until sugar dissolves. Bring to the boil. Reduce heat; simmer, uncovered, without stirring, 5 minutes. Gently stir in 4 cups cornflakes. Spread mixture into pan; press firmly. Refrigerate about 30 minutes or until set. Spread 350g (11 ounces) melted milk eating chocolate over slice; stand at room temperature until set.

prep + cook time 30 minutes (+ refrigeration) **makes** 24

honey and coconut muesli bars >

Preheat oven to 160°C/325°F. Grease 23cm x 32cm (9 inch x 13 inch) swiss roll pan; line base and long sides with baking paper, extending paper 5cm (2 inches) over sides. Combine 2½ cups rolled oats, 1 cup rice bubbles, ½ cup shredded coconut, ½ cup slivered almonds, 1 tablespoon honey and 395g (14 ounces) canned sweetened condensed milk in large bowl; press mixture firmly into pan. Bake about 40 minutes or until browned lightly. Cool in pan.

prep + cook time 50 minutes **makes** 36

< white chocolate and berry cheesecake slice

Grease deep 20cm (8 inch) square loose-based cake pan. Place 250g (8 ounces) butternut snap biscuits in base of pan. Sprinkle 2 teaspoons gelatine over ¼ cup boiling water in small heatproof jug; stand jug in small saucepan of simmering water, stir until gelatine dissolves. Cool 5 minutes. Meanwhile, beat 375g (12 ounces) softened cream cheese and ⅓ cup caster (superfine) sugar in small bowl with electric mixer until smooth; beat in 1¼ cups (300ml) pouring cream. Stir in the gelatine mixture, 185g (6 ounces) melted white eating chocolate and 125g (4 ounces) frozen mixed berries. Pour filling into pan; sprinkle with another 90g (3 ounces) frozen mixed berries. Refrigerate 3 hours or overnight.

prep time 30 minutes (+ refrigeration) **makes** 20

lattice slice with passionfruit icing

2 teaspoons gelatine
2 tablespoons water
250g (8 ounces) cream cheese, softened
250g (8 ounces) unsalted butter, softened
½ cup (110g) caster (superfine) sugar
1 teaspoon vanilla extract
2 tablespoons lemon juice
35 square lattice biscuits (350g) (see notes)
PASSIONFRUIT ICING
2 cups (320g) icing (confectioners') sugar
2 teaspoons unsalted butter
2 tablespoons passionfruit pulp
2 teaspoons hot water, approximately

1 Grease 20cm x 30cm (8 inch x 12 inch) rectangular pan; line base and long sides with baking paper, extending paper 5cm (2 inches) over sides.
2 Sprinkle gelatine over the water in small heatproof jug; stand jug in small saucepan of simmering water, stir until gelatine dissolves.

3 Beat cream cheese, butter, sugar and extract in small bowl with electric mixer until smooth. Stir in juice and gelatine mixture.
4 Line base of pan with half the biscuits; trim biscuits to fit, if necessary. Spread cream cheese filling evenly over biscuit base; top with remaining biscuits.
5 Make passionfruit icing.
6 Spread passionfruit icing over biscuits. Refrigerate 3 hours or overnight.

PASSIONFRUIT ICING Sift icing sugar into small heatproof bowl; stir in butter, passionfruit and enough of the water to make a thick paste. Place bowl over small saucepan of simmering water; stir until icing is spreadable.

prep time 30 minutes (+ refrigeration) **makes** 12
notes You need to buy 2 packets of lattice biscuits for this recipe. The slice will keep in an airtight container in the fridge for up to four days.

rocky road slice

250g (8 ounces) plain chocolate biscuits
125g (4 ounces) butter, melted
250g (8 ounces) dark eating chocolate,
  chopped coarsely
45g (1½ ounces) butter, chopped coarsely
½ cup (70g) coarsely chopped roasted
  unsalted peanuts
⅔ cup (50g) shredded coconut
250g (8 ounces) white eating chocolate, melted
220g (7 ounces) white marshmallows,
  chopped coarsely

1 Grease deep 23cm (9 inch) square cake pan;
line base and sides with baking paper, extending
paper 5cm (2 inches) over sides.
2 Process biscuits until fine; add melted butter,
process until combined. Press mixture over base
of pan. Refrigerate about 20 minutes or until firm.
3 Stir dark chocolate and chopped butter in small
saucepan over low heat until smooth. Remove from
heat; stir in peanuts and coconut, spread mixture over
base. Refrigerate about 30 minutes or until firm.
4 Combine white chocolate and marshmallows in
medium bowl; spread marshmallow mixture over nut
layer. Refrigerate about 1 hour or until firm.
prep + cook time 20 minutes (+ refrigeration)
makes 24
note Slice will keep in an airtight container in the
fridge for up to a week.

apple streusel slice

220g (7 ounces) unsalted butter, softened
1 cup (220g) caster (superfine) sugar
2 egg yolks
1⅓ cups (200g) plain (all-purpose) flour
½ cup (75g) self-raising flour
2 tablespoons custard powder
4 large apples (800g), sliced thinly
1 tablespoon honey
1 teaspoon finely grated lemon rind
STREUSEL TOPPING
½ cup (75g) plain (all-purpose) flour
¼ cup (35g) self-raising flour
⅓ cup (75g) firmly packed light brown sugar
½ teaspoon ground cinnamon
90g (3 ounces) unsalted butter, chopped coarsely

1 Make streusel topping.
2 Preheat oven to 180°C/350°F. Grease 20cm x 30cm (8 inch x 12 inch) rectangular pan; line base and long sides with baking paper, extending paper 5cm (2 inches) over sides.
3 Beat butter, sugar and egg yolks in small bowl with electric mixer until light and fluffy, transfer to large bowl; stir in sifted flours and custard powder. Press mixture into pan; bake 25 minutes. Cool 15 minutes.
4 Meanwhile, cook apple, honey and rind, covered, in medium saucepan, stirring occasionally, about 5 minutes or until apples are tender. Remove from heat; drain, cool 15 minutes.
5 Spread apple mixture over base; coarsely grate streusel topping over apple. Bake about 20 minutes. Cool slice in pan.
STREUSEL TOPPING Process ingredients until combined. Enclose in plastic wrap; freeze 1 hour or until firm.

prep + cook time 1 hour (+ freezing and cooling)
makes 12
note Slice will keep in an airtight container in the fridge for up to three days.

bakewell slice

155g (5 ounces) unsalted butter, softened
¼ cup (55g) caster (superfine) sugar
2 egg yolks
1½ cups (225g) plain (all-purpose) flour
¾ cup (90g) ground almonds
¾ cup (240g) strawberry jam (conserve)
ALMOND FILLING
185g (6 ounces) unsalted butter, softened
1 teaspoon finely grated lemon rind
¾ cup (165g) caster (superfine) sugar
3 eggs
1¼ cups (150g) ground almonds
¼ cup (35g) plain (all-purpose) flour
LEMON ICING
2 cups (320g) icing (confectioners') sugar
¼ cup (60ml) lemon juice, approximately

1 Beat butter, sugar and egg yolks in small bowl with electric mixer until combined. Stir in sifted flour and ground almonds, in two batches. Knead pastry gently on floured surface until smooth. Enclose in plastic wrap; refrigerate 30 minutes.
2 Make almond filling.
3 Meanwhile, preheat oven to 200°C/400°F.
4 Grease 20cm x 30cm (8 inch x 12 inch) rectangular pan; line base and long sides with baking paper, extending paper 5cm (2 inches) over sides. Roll out pastry between sheets of baking paper until large enough to line pan; press into base and sides, trim edge. Spread jam then almond filling evenly over base. Bake about 30 minutes. Cool in pan.
5 Make lemon icing.
6 Spread lemon icing over slice; stand at room temperature until icing is set.
ALMOND FILLING Beat butter, rind and sugar in small bowl with electric mixer until light and fluffy. Beat in eggs, one at a time. Stir in ground almonds and sifted flour.
LEMON ICING Sift icing sugar into small bowl; stir in enough of the juice until icing is spreadable.
prep + cook time 1 hour 10 minutes
(+ refrigeration and standing) **makes** 32
note Slice can be stored in an airtight container for up to a week.

fruit mince slice

1½ cups (225g) plain (all-purpose) flour
1¼ cups (185g) self-raising flour
155g (5 ounces) cold butter, chopped
1 tablespoon golden syrup or treacle
1 egg
⅓ cup (80ml) milk, approximately
2 teaspoons milk, extra
1 tablespoon demerara sugar
FRUIT MINCE
500g (1 pound) mixed dried fruit, chopped coarsely
½ cup (125ml) water
½ cup (110g) firmly packed dark brown sugar
1 tablespoon orange marmalade
2 teaspoons finely grated orange rind
2 tablespoons orange juice

1 Make fruit mince.
2 Grease 20cm x 30cm (8 inch x 12 inch) rectangular pan; line base and long sides with baking paper, extending paper 5cm (2 inches) over sides.
3 Sift flours into large bowl; rub in butter until mixture is crumbly. Stir in combined syrup and egg and enough milk to make a firm dough. Knead dough gently on floured surface until smooth. Refrigerate 30 minutes.
4 Preheat oven to 200°C/400°F.
5 Divide dough in half. Roll one half between sheets of baking paper until large enough to cover base of pan; press into pan, spread fruit mince over dough.
6 Roll remaining dough between sheets of baking paper until large enough to cover fruit mince; place on top of fruit mince, trim to fit. Brush with extra milk; sprinkle with demerara sugar. Bake about 20 minutes. Cool in pan before cutting.
FRUIT MINCE Combine ingredients in medium saucepan; cook, stirring, over medium heat, about 10 minutes or until thick. Cool.

prep + cook time 50 minutes
(+ refrigeration and cooling) **makes** 24
notes Use white (granulated) sugar instead of the demerara, if you like. Slice can be stored in an airtight container for up to a week.

apricot choc-aroon slice >

Preheat oven to 150°C/300°F. Grease 20cm x 30cm (8 inch x 12 inch) rectangular pan; line base and long sides with baking paper, extending paper 5cm (2 inches) over sides. Beat 3 egg whites in small bowl with electric mixer until soft peaks form; gradually add ½ cup caster (superfine) sugar, beating until sugar dissolves. Fold in ¼ cup plain (all-purpose) flour, 1⅓ cups shredded coconut, ½ cup finely chopped dried apricots and 90g (3 ounces) coarsely grated milk eating chocolate. Spread mixture into pan; bake 15 minutes. Sprinkle slice with ½ cup slivered almonds, press down gently; bake about 30 minutes or until browned lightly. Cool in pan. Drizzle slice with 90g (3 ounces) melted milk eating chocolate; stand at room temperature until set.
prep + cook time 1 hour (+ cooling) **makes** 30

< blueberry, lime and passionfruit slice

Preheat oven to 180°C/350°F. Grease 20cm x 30cm (8 inch x 12 inch) rectangular pan; line base and long sides with baking paper, extending paper 5cm (2 inches) over sides. Whisk 6 egg whites in large bowl until frothy; stir in 1½ cups ground almonds, 1½ cups icing (confectioners') sugar, ¼ cup plain (all-purpose) flour, ¼ cup self-raising flour, ½ cup desiccated coconut, 155g (5 ounces) melted butter and 2 teaspoons finely grated lime rind. Pour mixture into pan; sprinkle with 155g (5 ounces) fresh or frozen blueberries, drizzle with ¼ cup passionfruit pulp. Bake about 1¼ hours; stand slice in pan 10 minutes before turning, top-side up, onto wire rack to cool. Cut into rectangles; dust with sifted icing sugar to serve.
prep + cook time 1 hour 40 minutes **makes** 16

white Christmas slice >

Grease 20cm x 30cm (8 inch x 12 inch) rectangular
pan; line base and long sides with baking paper,
extending paper 5cm (2 inches) over sides. Melt 500g
(1 pound) coarsely chopped white eating chocolate
in large heatproof bowl set over large saucepan of
simmering water (do not let water touch base of
bowl). Remove from heat; quickly stir in 1 cup rice
bubbles, 1 cup sultanas, 1 cup desiccated coconut,
⅔ cup finely chopped dried apricots and ½ cup halved
red glacé cherries. Press mixture firmly into pan.
Refrigerate 2 hours or until firm.
prep time 20 minutes (+ refrigeration) **makes** 32

< lime and coconut slice

Grease 20cm x 30cm (8 inch x 12 inch) rectangular pan; line
base and long sides with baking paper, extending paper
5cm (2 inches) over sides. Process 185g (6 ounces) plain
sweet biscuits until fine. Chop 60g (2 ounces) extra plain
sweet biscuits coarsely. Combine ½ cup sweetened
condensed milk and 90g (3 ounces) chopped unsalted
butter in small saucepan; stir over medium heat until
smooth. Combine processed and chopped biscuits,
1 teaspoon finely grated lime rind, 1 tablespoon lime
juice and ½ cup shredded coconut in medium bowl. Add
condensed milk mixture; stir to combine. Press mixture
firmly into pan. Refrigerate 30 minutes or until firm.
Meanwhile, sift 2 cups icing (confectioners') sugar into
small heatproof bowl; stir in 15g (½ ounce) melted unsalted
butter, 2 tablespoons lime juice and enough water to make
a thick paste. Place bowl over small saucepan of simmering
water, stir until icing is spreadable; spread icing over slice.
Refrigerate 30 minutes or until firm.
prep + cook time 25 minutes (+ refrigeration)
makes 24

double-chocolate slice

125g (4 ounces) butter, chopped coarsely
1 cup (220g) firmly packed dark brown sugar
185g (6 ounces) dark eating chocolate
1¼ cups (110g) rolled oats
¾ cup (75g) coarsely chopped walnuts
1 egg
¾ cup (110g) plain (all-purpose) flour
¼ cup (35g) self-raising flour
½ teaspoon bicarbonate of soda (baking soda)
⅔ cup (130g) dark Choc Bits

1 Preheat oven to 160°C/325°F. Grease 20cm x 30cm (8 inch x 12 inch) rectangular pan; line base and long sides with baking paper, extending paper 5cm (2 inches) over sides.
2 Melt butter in medium saucepan over low heat. Remove from heat; stir in sugar until smooth.
3 Coarsely chop half the chocolate.
4 Stir oats and nuts into butter mixture, then egg, sifted dry ingredients, chopped chocolate and Choc Bits.
5 Spread mixture evenly into pan. Bake about 30 minutes. Cover hot slice with foil; cool.
6 Melt remaining chocolate. Turn slice, top-side-up, onto wire rack; drizzle with chocolate. Stand at room temperature until set before cutting.
prep + cook time 45 minutes
(+ cooling and standing) **makes** 30
note Slice can be stored in an airtight container for up to a week.

marzipan chocolate and cranberry slice

500g (1 pound) marzipan
500g (1 pound) dark eating (semi-sweet)
   chocolate, chopped coarsely
1¼ cups (300ml) thickened (heavy) cream
1 tablespoon finely grated orange rind
1¼ cups (165g) dried cranberries,
   chopped coarsely
250g (8 ounces) milk eating chocolate,
   chopped coarsely
2 teaspoons vegetable oil

1 Grease 20cm x 30cm (8 inch x 12 inch) rectangular pan; line base and long sides with baking paper, extending paper 5cm (2 inches) over sides.
2 Roll marzipan between sheets of baking paper until large enough to cover base of pan; press into pan.
3 Combine dark chocolate, cream and rind in medium saucepan; stir over low heat until smooth. Stir in cranberries. Cool 10 minutes.
4 Pour chocolate mixture over marzipan base. Refrigerate 2 hours.
5 Combine milk chocolate and oil in small heatproof bowl; stir over small saucepan of simmering water until smooth. Cool 10 minutes.
6 Pour milk chocolate mixture over dark chocolate filling. Refrigerate 3 hours or overnight.
prep + cook time 25 minutes (+ refrigeration)
makes 24
note Slice will keep in an airtight container in the fridge for up to a week.

rum ball slice

⅓ cup (50g) plain (all-purpose) flour
⅓ cup (50g) self-raising flour
2 tablespoons cocoa powder
½ cup (40g) desiccated coconut
¾ cup (165g) firmly packed dark brown sugar
125g (4 ounces) unsalted butter, melted
1¼ cups (300ml) pouring cream
375g (12 ounces) dark eating chocolate,
   chopped coarsely
RUM BALLS
3 cups (450g) plain cake crumbs
⅓ cup (110g) apricot jam (conserve),
   warmed, strained
¼ cup (25g) cocoa powder
2 tablespoons dark rum

1 Preheat oven to 180°C/350°F. Grease 20cm x 30cm (8 inch x 12 inch) rectangular pan; line base and long sides with baking paper, extending paper 5cm (2 inches) over sides.
2 Combine sifted flours, cocoa, coconut, sugar and butter in medium bowl; press mixture evenly over base of pan. Bake about 20 minutes. Cool.
3 Meanwhile, make rum balls.
4 To make ganache, bring cream to the boil in small saucepan. Remove from heat; pour over chocolate in medium heatproof bowl, stir until smooth. Cool 10 minutes.
5 Spread ½ cup of the ganache over base; top evenly with rum balls. Spoon remaining ganache over rum balls. Refrigerate 3 hours or overnight.
RUM BALLS Combine ingredients in medium bowl. Roll level teaspoons of mixture into balls.
prep + cook time 50 minutes
(+ cooling and refrigeration) **makes** 36
note Slice will keep in an airtight container in the fridge for up to a week.

chocolate coconut rough slice

⅓ cup (50g) self-raising flour
⅓ cup (50g) plain (all-purpose) flour
2 tablespoons cocoa powder
⅔ cup (50g) desiccated coconut
¾ cup (165g) firmly packed light brown sugar
90g (3 ounces) unsalted butter, melted
250g (8 ounces) milk eating chocolate, melted
COCONUT ROUGH FILLING
1½ cups (240g) icing (confectioners') sugar
1½ cups (120g) desiccated coconut
2 tablespoons cocoa powder
⅔ cup (160ml) sweetened condensed milk
75g (2½ ounces) unsalted butter, melted
1 teaspoon vanilla extract

1 Preheat oven to 180°C/350°F. Grease 20cm x 30cm (8 inch x 12 inch) rectangular pan; line base and long sides with baking paper, extending paper 5cm (2 inches) over sides.
2 Combine sifted flours and cocoa, coconut, sugar and butter in medium bowl; press mixture evenly over base of pan. Bake about 20 minutes. Cool 15 minutes.
3 Meanwhile, make coconut rough filling.
4 Spread filling evenly over warm base; top with melted chocolate. Refrigerate 2 hours or until firm.
COCONUT ROUGH FILLING Combine ingredients in medium bowl.
prep + cook time 45 minutes
(+ cooling and refrigeration) **makes** 16
note Slice can be stored in an airtight container for up to a week.

florentine slice >

Grease 20cm x 30cm (8 inch x 12 inch) rectangular pan; line base and long sides with baking paper, extending paper 5cm (2 inches) over sides. Combine 395g (14 ounces) canned sweetened condensed milk and 90g (3 ounces) chopped unsalted butter in medium saucepan; stir over medium heat until smooth. Combine 3 cups lightly crushed corn flakes, ¾ cup roasted flaked almonds, ¾ cup sultanas, ½ cup coarsely chopped roasted macadamia nuts, ½ cup halved red glacé cherries and ⅓ cup currants in large bowl. Stir in condensed milk mixture. Spread 250g (8 ounces) melted dark eating (semi-sweet) chocolate over base of pan; top with corn flake mixture. Refrigerate 3 hours or until firm.

prep + cook time 25 minutes (+ refrigeration)
makes 15

< hedgehog slice

Grease 20cm x 30cm (8 inch x 12 inch) rectangular pan; line base and long sides with baking paper, extending paper 5cm (2 inches) over sides. Combine 395g (14 ounces) canned sweetened condensed milk and 90g (3 ounces) chopped unsalted butter in medium saucepan; stir over medium heat until smooth. Remove from heat; add 185g (6 ounces) chopped dark eating (semi-sweet) chocolate, stir until smooth. Break 250g (8 ounces) plain sweet biscuits into small pieces; place in large bowl with ⅔ cup roasted hazelnuts and ⅔ cup sultanas. Stir in chocolate mixture. Press mixture firmly into pan. Refrigerate 2 hours or until firm.

prep + cook time 20 minutes (+ refrigeration)
makes 20
note We used plain sweet shortbread biscuits.

marshmallow rice bubble slice >

Grease 20cm x 30cm (8 inch x 12 inch) rectangular pan; line base and long sides with baking paper, extending paper 5cm (2 inches) over sides. Combine 250g (8 ounces) vanilla and raspberry marshmallows and 90g (3 ounces) chopped unsalted butter in medium saucepan; stir over medium heat until smooth. Place 4 cups rice bubbles and half 155g (5 ounce) tub rainbow chocolate chips in large bowl; add marshmallow mixture, stir until smooth. Using wet hand, press mixture firmly into pan; sprinkle with remaining rainbow chocolate chips. Refrigerate 2 hours or until firm.
prep + cook time 15 minutes (+ refrigeration)
makes 40

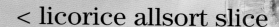

< licorice allsort slice

Grease 20cm x 30cm (8 inch x 12 inch) rectangular pan; line base and long sides with baking paper, extending paper 5cm (2 inches) over sides. Process 185g (6 ounces) plain sweet biscuits until fine. Chop 60g (2 ounces) extra plain sweet biscuits coarsely. Combine ½ cup sweetened condensed milk and 90g (3 ounces) chopped unsalted butter in small saucepan; stir over medium heat until smooth. Combine processed and chopped biscuits with 155g (5 ounces) coarsely chopped licorice allsorts in medium bowl. Stir in condensed milk mixture. Press mixture firmly into pan. Refrigerate 30 minutes or until firm. Meanwhile, combine 250g (8 ounces) coarsely chopped milk eating chocolate and 2 teaspoons vegetable oil in small heatproof bowl, stir over saucepan of simmering water until smooth; spread chocolate mixture over slice. Refrigerate 30 minutes or until firm.
prep + cook time 25 minutes (+ refrigeration)
makes 15

Glossary

ALLSPICE also known as pimento or jamaican pepper; so-named because it tastes like a combination of nutmeg, cumin, clove and cinnamon – all spices. It is available whole (a pea-sized dark-brown berry) or ground, and used in both sweet and savoury dishes.

ALMONDS
blanched whole nuts with brown skins removed.
essence also known as extract.
ground also known as almond meal; nuts are powdered to a coarse flour-like texture.

BAKING PAPER also parchment paper or baking parchment – is a silicone-coated paper that is primarily used for lining baking pans and oven trays so cakes and biscuits won't stick, making removal easy.

BICARBONATE OF SODA also known as baking or carb soda; a raising agent used in baking.

BISCUITS also known as cookies.
butternut snap crunchy cookie made with golden syrup, oats and coconut.
chocolate wheaten wheatmeal-based biscuit, topped with milk or dark chocolate.
lattice an open-weave square-shaped biscuit. These flaky pastry biscuits are made from flour, oil, sugar and milk powder. The dough is gently rolled into very fine sheets, just like flaky pastry, and is then glazed with a light sprinkling of sugar before being baked until puffed and golden.
plain chocolate a crisp sweet biscuit with added cocoa powder but having no icing or filling.
plain sweet a crisp sweet biscuit without icing or any fillings.
shortbread a pale golden, crumbly, buttery-tasting cookie made with just three ingredients: butter, sugar and flour (generally one part sugar, two parts butter and three parts flour).
Tim Tam chocolate biscuits coated in melted chocolate; made from chocolate, flour, sugar, oil, golden syrup, milk powder and cocoa.

BUTTER use salted or unsalted (sweet) butter; 125g is equal to one stick (4 ounces) of butter.
unsalted butter often called 'sweet' butter, simply has no added salt. It is mainly used in baking.

CARAMEL TOP 'N' FILL a caramel filling made from milk and cane sugar. Can be used straight from the can for cheesecakes, slices and tarts. Is similar to sweetened condensed milk, only has a thicker, caramel consistency.

CHEWY TOFFEES rectangular-shaped toffees with a creamy buttery taste; they are chewy rather than hard in texture.

CHOCOLATE
chocolate-hazelnut spread we use Nutella. Originally developed when chocolate was in short supply during World War 2, so hazelnuts were added to the chocolate to increase supply.
dark eating also known as semi-sweet or luxury chocolate; made of a high percentage of cocoa liquor and cocoa butter, and a little added sugar. Unless stated otherwise, we use dark eating chocolate in this book.
freckles small chocolate discs covered with hundreds and thousands.
milk eating the most popular eating chocolate, mild and very sweet; similar to dark with the difference being the addition of milk solids.
peppermint cream a confectionery with a peppermint fondant centre that is covered in dark chocolate.
peppermint crisp a chocolate bar with a crisp peppermint centre covered with dark chocolate.
white eating contains no cocoa solids but derives its sweet flavour from cocoa butter. Is very sensitive to heat, so watch carefully when melting.

CINNAMON dried inner bark of the shoots of the cinnamon tree; available in stick (quill) or ground form.

CLOVES dried flower buds of a tropical tree; can be used whole or in ground form. Has a distinctively pungent and 'spicy' scent and flavour.

COCOA POWDER also known as cocoa; dried, unsweetened, roasted then ground cocoa beans (cacao seeds).

CORN FLAKES a commercially manufactured cereal made of dehydrated, then baked crisp flakes of corn. Also available as a prepared, finely ground mixture used for coating or crumbing food before frying.

CORNFLOUR also known as cornstarch; used as a thickening agent. Available as 100% corn (maize) and wheaten cornflour.

CREAM we used fresh cream, also known as pure cream and pouring cream, unless otherwise stated. Has no additives. Minimum fat content 35%.
thickened a whipping cream containing a thickener. Minimum fat content 35%.

CREAM CHEESE commonly known as Philadelphia or Philly, a soft cows'-milk cheese with a fat content of at least 33%. Sold at supermarkets in bulk or in smaller-sized packages.

CREAM OF TARTAR the acid ingredient in baking powder; added to confectionery mixtures to help prevent sugar from crystallising. Keeps frostings creamy and improves volume when beating egg whites.

CUSTARD POWDER instant mixture used to make pouring custard; it is similar to North American instant pudding mixes.

FLOUR
plain an all-purpose flour made from wheat.
rice a very fine flour made from ground white rice.
self-raising plain flour that has been sifted with baking powder in the proportion of 1 cup flour to 2 teaspoons baking powder.
wholemeal milled from whole wheat grain (bran, germ and endosperm). Available as plain or self-raising.

FOOD COLOURING dyes that can be used to change the colour of various foods. These dyes can be eaten and do not change the taste to a noticeable extent.

FRUIT, GLACÉ have been preserved by boiling in a heavy sugar syrup.

GELATINE if using gelatine leaves, three teaspoons of powdered gelatine (8g or one sachet) is roughly equivalent to four gelatine leaves.

GINGER, GROUND also known as powdered ginger; used as a flavouring in cakes, pies and puddings but cannot be substituted for fresh ginger.

GOLDEN SYRUP a by-product of refined sugarcane; pure maple syrup or honey can be substituted.

HAZELNUTS, GROUND nuts have been ground into a coarse or fine powder. Also known as hazelnut meal.

JAM also known as preserve or conserve; most often made from fruit.

JERSEY CARAMELS two layers of sweet condensed milk caramel that sandwiches a layer of white caramel. Soft, chewy and sweet.

LIQUEURS
coconut-flavoured we used Malibu, but you can use your favourite coconut-flavoured liqueur.
hazelnut-flavoured we used Frangelico, but you can use your favourite brand.
limoncello a digestive (an alcoholic drink that is used to stimulate or assist digestion; usually taken at the end of the meal). Made from the peel only of fragrant lemons. The peels are steeped in a good-quality clear alcohol then diluted with sugar and water.
orange-flavoured we used Curacao or Grand Marnier, but you can use your favourite brand.

MALTED MILK POWDER a combination of wheat flour, malt flour and milk, which are evaporated to give the powder its fine appearance and to make it easily absorbable in liquids.

MARMALADE a preserve, usually based on citrus fruit.

MARZIPAN is an almond and sugar paste used to cover cakes, or sculpted into a variety of shapes to be eaten as candy or used as cake decorations.

MILK
full-cream milk powder evaporated milk concentrate, containing about 40% milk solids. Is dried to reduce the moisture content to about 3% and to prevent particles from clumping.
sweetened condensed milk from which 60% of the water has been removed; the remaining milk is then sweetened with sugar.

MIXED SPICE a blend of ground spices usually consisting of cinnamon, allspice and nutmeg.

NUTMEG the dried nut of an evergreen tree native to Indonesia; it is available in ground form or you can grate your own with a fine grater.

OATS
quick cooking oats are generally thinner than rolled oats, so absorb more water and cook faster.
rolled oats are oat groats (oats that have been husked) steamed-softened, flattened, dried and packaged for consumption as a cereal product.

ORANGE BLOSSOM WATER also known as orange flower water; a concentrated flavouring made from orange blossoms. Available from Middle-Eastern food stores and some supermarkets and delicatessens. Can't be substituted with citrus flavourings as the taste is completely different.

PASTRY
ready-rolled puff packaged sheets of frozen puff pastry, available from supermarkets.
ready-rolled shortcrust packaged sheets of shortcrust pastry, available from supermarkets. May come in sweet or savoury varieties.

PEANUT BUTTER peanuts ground to a paste; available in crunchy and smooth varieties.

PEANUTS not, in fact, a nut but the pod of a legume; also known as ground nut.

PEPPERMINT EXTRACT is distilled from the essential oils of peppermint leaves. Commonly used in cooking.

PLAIN CAKE CRUMBS any day-old cake, usually a dense butter (pound) cake is used. Can be chocolate cake crumbs, if the recipe calls for it.

PUMPKIN SEED KERNELS also known as pepitas.

RICE BUBBLES puffed rice breakfast cereal.

ROLLED OATS see oats.

ROSEWATER distilled from rose petals, and used in the Middle East, North Africa and India to flavour desserts. Don't confuse with rose essence, which is more concentrated.

SUGAR
caster also known as superfine or finely granulated table sugar.
dark brown a moist, dark brown sugar with a rich, distinctive, full flavour coming from natural molasses syrup.
demerara a granulated, golden coloured sugar with a distinctive rich flavour; often used to sweeten coffee.
icing also known as confectioners' sugar or powdered sugar; granulated sugar crushed together with a little added cornflour.
icing pure also known as confectioners' sugar or powdered sugar, but has no added cornflour.
light brown an extremely soft, finely granulated sugar retaining molasses for its characteristic colour and flavour.
white a coarse, granulated table sugar, also known as crystal sugar.

SUNFLOWER SEED KERNELS dried husked sunflower seeds.

SWEETENED CONDENSED MILK see milk.

TREACLE a concentrated, refined sugar syrup with a distinctive flavour and dark black colour.

WHEAT GERM the germ is where the seed germinates to form the sprout that becomes wheat. It has a nutty flavour and is very oily, which causes it to turn rancid quickly, so is usually removed during milling. It is available from health-food stores and supermarkets.

Conversion Chart

MEASURES

One Australian metric measuring cup holds approximately 250ml; one Australian metric tablespoon holds 20ml; one Australian metric teaspoon holds 5ml.

The difference between one country's measuring cups and another's is within a two- or three-teaspoon variance, and will not affect your cooking results. North America, New Zealand and the United Kingdom use a 15ml tablespoon.

All cup and spoon measurements are level. The most accurate way of measuring dry ingredients is to weigh them. When measuring liquids, use a clear glass or plastic jug with metric markings.

We use large eggs with an average weight of 60g.

DRY MEASURES

METRIC	IMPERIAL
15g	½oz
30g	1oz
60g	2oz
90g	3oz
125g	4oz (¼lb)
155g	5oz
185g	6oz
220g	7oz
250g	8oz (½lb)
280g	9oz
315g	10oz
345g	11oz
375g	12oz (¾lb)
410g	13oz
440g	14oz
470g	15oz
500g	16oz (1lb)
750g	24oz (1½lb)
1kg	32oz (2lb)

LIQUID MEASURES

METRIC	IMPERIAL
30ml	1 fluid oz
60ml	2 fluid oz
100ml	3 fluid oz
125ml	4 fluid oz
150ml	5 fluid oz (¼ pint)
190ml	6 fluid oz
250ml	8 fluid oz
300ml	10 fluid oz (½ pint)
500ml	16 fluid oz
600ml	20 fluid oz (1 pint)
1000ml (1 litre)	1¾ pints

LENGTH MEASURES

METRIC	IMPERIAL
3mm	⅛in
6mm	¼in
1cm	½in
2cm	¾in
2.5cm	1in
5cm	2in
6cm	2½in
8cm	3in
10cm	4in
13cm	5in
15cm	6in
18cm	7in
20cm	8in
23cm	9in
25cm	10in
28cm	11in
30cm	12in (1ft)

OVEN TEMPERATURES

These oven temperatures are only a guide for conventional ovens. For fan-forced ovens, check the manufacturer's manual.

	°C (CELSIUS)	°F (FAHRENHEIT)	GAS MARK
Very slow	120	250	½
Slow	150	275-300	1-2
Moderately slow	160	325	3
Moderate	180	350-375	4-5
Moderately hot	200	400	6
Hot	220	425-450	7-8
Very hot	240	475	9

Index

Published in 2010 by ACP Books, Sydney

ACP Books are published by ACP Magazines

a division of PBL Media Pty Limited

ACP BOOKS

General manager Christine Whiston
Editor-in-chief Susan Tomnay
Creative director & designer Hieu Chi Nguyen
Art director Hannah Blackmore
Senior editor Wendy Bryant
Food director Pamela Clark
Recipe development Rebecca Squadrito, Nicole Jennings
Sales & rights director Brian Cearnes
Marketing manager Bridget Cody
Senior business analyst Rebecca Varela
Circulation manager Jama Mclean
Operations manager David Scotto
Production manager Victoria Jefferys

Published by ACP Books, a division of ACP Magazines Ltd,
54 Park St, Sydney; GPO Box 4088, Sydney, NSW 2001.
phone (02) 9282 8618; fax (02) 9267 9438.
acpbooks@acpmagazines.com.au;
www.acpbooks.com.au

Printed by Toppan Printing Co, China.

United Kingdom Distributed by Australian Consolidated Press (UK),
phone (01604) 642 200; fax (01604) 642 300; books@acpuk.com

Macaroons and biscuits / food director Pamela Clark.
ISBN: 978 186396 937 6 (pbk.)
Notes: Includes index.
Subjects: Cookies. Cookery.
Other Authors/Contributors: Clark, Pamela.
Also Titled: Australian women's weekly.
Dewey Number: 641.8654
© ACP Magazines Ltd 2010
ABN 18 053 273 546

Photographer John Paul Urizar
Stylists Michaela Le Compte, Yael Gringham
Food preparation Elisabeth Macri

Scanpan cookware is used in the AWW Test Kitchen.

Send recipe enquiries to: recipeenquiries@acpmagazines.com.au